PRIMARY SCHOOL TEACHERS' SKILLS TO HELP DYSCALCULIC CHILDREN

PRIMARY SCHOOL TEACHERS' SKILLS TO HELP DYSCALCULIC CHILDREN

Dr. T. GEETHA
Dr. N. JAYA

KALPAZ

Primary School Teachers' Skills to Help Dyscalculic Children

ISBN: 81-7835-689-9

Dr. T. Geetha
Dr. N. Jaya

Published in 2009 in India by
Kalpaz Publications
C-30, Satyawati Nagar
Delhi - 110052
e-mail : Kalpaz@hotmail.com
Phone : 9212729499

Lesertype setting : Jai Vinayak Enterprises
Printed at : G. Print Process, Delhi

Contents

List of Tables

List of Figures

List of Plates

Preface

Development of human resources is the first step for the rapid improvement of any progressive society. It is through education of its children that a nation transmits heritage, recreates its culture, strengthens its economy and ensures its values. Education refines sensitivities and achievements of individuals. Hence it is right to consider that education is the potential instrument for human resource development.

Cognizing this aspect desirably, Article 45 of the Constitution provides education to all the children of the country. A variety of new challenges made it imperative to evolve new policy directions in the context of contemporary realities and future perspectives and hence the emergence of the National Policy on Education (NPE) in 1986.

Among the many reasons attributed for the inability to achieve the goal of Universal Elementary Education (UEE), is the poor retention Capacity of children in the education system. A UNICEF (1994) study reveals that only 52 per cent of enrolled primary school children reach Grade V.

Academic failure, learning inefficiency, anxiety barriers, dismissals, expulsions, dropouts, reading retardation and a host of other problems are rampant on the educational scene and the percentage of failing students are on the increase. Among them are the learning disabled children, who performed particularly poorly at school despite having otherwise average or above average level of intellectual ability (Ahuja, 1996, Murthy, 1995 and Lewis et al., 1994). Sharma (1993) reports that one in ten school going children are learning disabled.

The National Joint Committee for Learning Disabilities (NJCLD, 1981) defined learning disability as a generic term that refers to heterogeneous group of disorders manifested by significant difficulties in the acquisition and use of listening, speaking, reading, writing, reasoning or mathematical abilities. These children have an educationally significant discrepancy between estimated intellectual potential and actual level of performance related to basic disorders in the learning processes. Specific types of learning disabilities include dyslexia (reading disability) dysgraphia (writing disability) and dyscalculia (arithmetic disability).

Dyscalculia refers to inability to calculate, problems with numbers and quantitative thinking. Dyscalculic children are reported to have difficulty in learning to count meaningfully, master cardinal and ordinal systems and visualize cluster of objects as groups. It is the most widely used term for disabilities in arithmetics. While the term "Acalculia" is used to refer to complete inability to use mathematical symbols and perform arithmetic computations, the term "Dyscalculia" is reserved for less severe problems in these areas.

Children with learning difficulties in arithmetic (Dyscalculics), go unnoticed and unrecognized in schools. They continue with the difficulties and as a result have difficulty in thinking, recording and communicating the elements and relationships involving quantity.

The current trend in education of children with disabilities is geared towards integration. It is therefore ideal to keep the children with scholastic backwardness in regular schools and equip the regular class teachers to identify each child's specific problems in learning. This would in turn, lead to referring the child and in correcting the problems without labeling with a diagnostic tag. In the context of "Education for All", such a preparation of regular primary teachers is a major milestone towards achieving this goal.

Against this backdrop the investigator designed this study on "Efficacy of Remedial Package in Augmenting Primary School Teachers' Skills To Help Dyscalculic Children". The objectives of the study were to:

1. Sensitize primary school teachers on learning disabilities childrens
2. Assess the academic performance of primary school children to identify dyscalculic children among the scholastically backward.
3. Evolve a remedial package for dyscalculic children
4. Use and evaluate the efficacy of the developed remedial package for the children in need.

Methodology:

The methodology for the present investigation involved:

(A) Sensitizing Primary School Teachers on Learning Disabilities Among Children

A survey among the local primary school teachers was found essential to assess their awareness on learning disability, using a questionnaire. Ensuring their co-operation, 150 teachers handling classes I to V from 30 schools were selected adopting the purposive sampling method.

The response of the selected teachers brought to light the need to educate them on learning disability. This necessitated organizing a one day **"Awareness Programme on Dyslexia Among Primary School Children"**, for heads of institutions, teachers and parents.

Forty-six per cent of the selected teachers were in the age range of 20-30 years. Among the teachers, 65 per cent were graduates and 29 per cent were post-graduates. Fifty-three per cent teachers had two to four years teaching experience and 47 per cent had four to eight years.

A five day orientation programme for the selected primary school teachers on **"Identification and Education of Learning Disabled Children"**, was arranged with a major focus on discussing and clarifying important issues related to learning difficulties among school going children. Nineteen primary school teachers participated in this programme. As part of the programme **"Instructional Materials"** aimed at providing the teachers an understanding of the concept of learning disability in a comprehensive manner were prepared and distributed.

(B) Identifying Dyscalculic Primary School Children

This part of the study probed into the following aspects :

1. Assessing academic achievement of primary school children

In order to comprehend the subject in which there are more low achievers, an assessment of academic achievement among (1442) primary school children was undertaken. Five Matriculation schools that extended co-operation were considered for the collection of data. From the records maintained in the schools, the marks of students from Classes I to V were looked into, to identify the subject with greater number of low achievers. This aspects of the study enabled the investigator to know that there were more number of children with difficulties in mathematics.

From the same group, 115 children were pinned down as low

achievers in mathematics based on their achievement in four consecutive tests viz., Ist and IInd mid-term quarterly and half yearly and based on teachers' judgement.

In order to assess the intellectual ability of the selected low achievers in mathematics (115) **Raven's Coloured Progressive Matrices Test (1993)** was administered. **Arithmetic Diagnostic Test for Primary School Children** developed and standardized by Ramaa **(1994)** was also used to diagnose specific difficulties in arithmetics encountered by the selected low achievers (N = 115) from classes I to V. The test covered three major areas viz., number concept, arithmetic process operations (addition, subtraction, multiplication and division) and arithmetic reasoning. **A Behavioural Checklist** developed and standardized by **Swarup and Mehta (1991)** was used to assess the behavioural characteristics of the selected children.

Among the 115 children from classes I to V earlier identified as low achievers in athematics and screened for arithmetic performance, 63 children were identified as probable dyscalculics. Of the 63 children identified, 27 were eliminated on the grounds of subnormal intelligence, underage and those with behaviour problems. Finally, only 36 children were selected for the study.

From the school medical records, consultation with class teachers and observation by the investigator, the identified children were found to be normal in visual and auditory performance and fulfilled all the criteria required to identify them as for the study.

(C) Using and Evaluating the Remedial Package Developed for Dyscalculic Children

To integrate and implement the remedial programme, the 36 children identified as dyscalculics were grouped into control and experimental groups (18 each). On identifying the areas of difficulty in the various arithmetic concepts learnt by the selected children in the classroom, an attempt was made by the investigator to use various teaching aids while introducing multiple intervention strategies through multi-sensory approach to impart the required skills in basic arithmetic concepts.

Since remediation was focused on the acquisition of specific difficulty encountered by the individual child, a minimum of 20 sittings and a maximum of 30 sittings of 90 minutes duration each for remediation was found adequate along with the teachers regular inputs.

To help children acquire practice and mastery of the various skills for increasing their rate of computation and accuracy, model, probes, were also administered during remediation to enable them gain adequate skill and confidence with computations. The acquisition of specific skills taught and learnt by the children was assessed by a post test administered using the same Arithmetic Diagnostic Test.

The investigator's experiences in working with these children and the teachers, aided in the preparation of a remedial package for primary school teachers for use with children having learning difficulties in arithmetics. The major aspects in the remedial package developed included the remedial approach implemented with teaching specific strategies, reading materials on the concept, characteristics, causes and problems of the learning disabled. Teaching methods and readiness for number instruction were also included.

The teacher / parent could also get access to details on specific strategies for effective instruction, play materials / resources for imparting arithmetic skills, general principles involved in instruction along with a set of games to impart various skills and 'model' probes for teachers' use.

The remedial package developed was evaluated by ten primary school teachers involved in teaching mathematics. A checklist was evolved for teachers to adjudge the efficacy of the package.

The uniqueness of the remedial instruction imparted was the introduction of realistic instructional activities using locally available resource materials that could challenge children to perceive, investigate and justify their computations.

Salient findings of the study

The findings of the study are presented below under three major dimensions :

(A) Sensitizing Primary School Teachers on Learning Disabilities Among Children

Prior to the sensitization programme for the teachers, their awareness on learning disabilities was assessed, the findings of which enlisted below:

1. Among the various terminologies used in referring to the learning disabled children, 50 per cent of the teachers perceived them as problem children in their classroom, 19 per cent as educationally backward and 12 per cent considered these children as slow learners.
2. Goal setting for an individual learning disabled as an important

pre-requisite in the teaching process was considered important by 37 per cent of selected teachers. Only one fourth of the selected teachers were aware of individual variation in the degree of learning to be considered as an important factor in planning individual remediation.

3. Participation in the orientation programme organized enabled the teachers to acquire adequate knowledge of the terminologies to refer to the children with learning disabilities. There was significant difference at one per cent level between the pre and post mean scores of teachers on their concept of learning disability.
4. Special remedial services in terms of individualized instruction, peer tutoring and the existence of dyslexic remedial training centres had limited awareness among teachers in the pre-training level (58%) while the post-training scores brought forth as much as 90 per cent of the teachers becoming familiar with the above issues. The difference in knowledge scores was significant at five per cent level.

(B) Identifying Dyscalculic Primary School Children

1. The achievement scores of 1442 children from five selected schools in four subject areas viz., English, Language, Science and Maths assessed and analysed revealed a higher percentage on an average (20%) of low achievers in mathematics, the percentage being more than 25 in classes II, IV and V.
2. Use of Raven's Progressive Matrices to assess the IQ of the selected group of low achievers in mathematics reflected that only 34 per cent children belonged to 'average intelligence' category while almost 41 per cent were grouped in 'below average intelligence' category. Low achievers (63) with average and above average intelligence and with failure in basic arithmetic skills in the arithmetic diagnostic test were considered dyscalculics.
3. An analysis of arithmetic errors committed by identified dyscalculics revealed that a little above 50 per cent of the children had difficulty to bring multiplication tables to memory. Writing the numbers mentioned (42%), wrong operations and problem solving (39%), reading digit wise (36%), spelling errors and difficulty with written symbols (28%) were observed.

A checklist assessing the teachers' reactions and perceptions of the remediation programme and its strategies indicated that they found them beneficial. The changes observed in every dyscalculic child (experimental group) and the results revealed that the intervention was worthwhile leading to moderate improvement.

(C) Use of Remedial Package for Dyscalculic Children

The use of remedial package (developed by the investigator) by the teachers over a period of three months with the 18 dyscalculic (experimental group) children revealed a significant improvement in the overall performance scores obtained on the Arithmetic Diagnostic Test administered after the remediation inputs. The mean scores for the experimental group in the pre-and post-test were 33 and 64 while those of the control group were 17 and 33 respectively.

The remediation inputs seem to have helped significantly in equipping children with necessary skills to overcome their difficulties in basic arithmetics. The study has also highlighted the need to orient teachers on this important problem area to arrest stagnation and repeated failure that might lead to drop outs at primary school level.

References

1. Ahuja, A. (1996). Visible Handicaps in the Act of Disabled, The Hindu, July 16th, p. 26.
2. Lewis, C., Hitch, G.J., and Walker, R.P. (1994). The Prevalence of Specific Arithmetic Difficulties and Specific Reading Difficulties in 9 to 10 year old Boys and Girls, Journal of Child Psychology and Psychiatry, 35(2), pp. 283-292.
3. Murthy, V.K. (1995). Slow Learning Children - A Review, The Hindu, April 18th, p. 26.
4. Ramaa, S. (1994). Arithmetic Diagnostic Test for Primary School Children, Mysore : Chetna Book House.
5. Raven, J.C. (1993). Coloured Progressive Matrices, London : E.T. Heron and Co. Ltd.
6. Sharma, G. (1993). Tackling Learning Disabilities, The Hindu, September 19th, p. IV.
7. Swarup, S. and Mehta, D.H. (1991). Behavioural Checklist for Screening the Learning Disabled, Bombay : SNDT Women's University.
8. UNICEF (1994). The Right to be a Child, UNICEF India Background Paper, New Delhi, p. 16.

Acknowledgements

The investigator records her reverential gratitude to the great Architect of this Temple of Learning our Chancellor Late. **Sri Avinashilingam Chettiar Avargal,** fondly remembered as **"Ayya Avargal"** for he was the source of inspiration for introducing Special Education as a field of study.

The investigator expresses her deep sense of gratitude and indebtedness to **Dr. (Mrs.) Rajammal P. Devadas, M.A., M.Sc.,Ph.D. (Ohio State), D.Sc. (Madras),** Chancellor, Avinashilingam Deemed University for the opportunity provided to pursue research in this new and emerging area of Special Education and also for the guidance given.

The investigator is deeply indebted to **Dr. (Mrs.) Lakshmi Santa Rajagopal, M.S. (Tennessee). Ph.D (Madras),** Vice-Chancellor, Avinashilingam Institute for Home Science and Higher Education for Women, Coimbatore, for her constant motivation, guidance and who has always been a source of inspiration in all my endeavours.

The investigator expresses her deep sense of gratitude to **Dr. (Mrs.) Saroja Prabhakaran, Registrar,** Avinashilingam Institute for Home Science and Higher Education for Women, Coimbatore, for all the infrastructural help rendered in the conduct of this study.

The researcher expresses her sincere thanks to **Dr. (Mrs.) Usha** Chandrasekar, Dean, Faculty of Home Science for the permission granted and encouragement offered in the conduct of this study.

The investigator records her indebtedness to her guide **Dr. (Mrs.) N. Jaya, M.Sc., Ph.D. (Madras),** Professor and Head, Department of Human Development without whose faith, forbearance and persistence this research would not have seen the light of this day. Her deep insight and sustained enthusiasm and concern, incessant guidance, bubbling energy and spirit of motivation significantly contributed towards the successful completion of this study.

For his gracious support in sharing and sparing his ideas,

experience, suggestions and time the investigator acknowledges with gratitude the guidance given by Dr. Coen, G.A., DeJong, Director, Bartimeus, The Netherlands, who is also a Visiting Professor in the Department of Human Development.

Genuine and concerned help and expertise from the Madras Dyslexia Association, Madras in gratefully appreciated and acknowledged.

The investigator remains ever grateful to the constructive suggestions and help rendered by all her collegues in the department and particularly thankful to (Mrs.) U. Saty Head Department of English, who has been especially helpful in sharing her ideas in editing.

The completion of this research would not have been possible without the active involvement, participation, and co-operation of the teachers and children from the selected schools. The investigator gratefully acknowledges their significant contribution.

The investigator also acknowledges the influences of her teachers in the various departments for having given their invaluable input of ideas and feedback at all stages towards the completion of the study.

1

Introduction

"The past is our foundation
The present our material
The future our aim and summit".

- Sri Aurobindo

Today the focus on education is sometimes on the past, very often on the present and seldom on the future.

Development of human resources is the first step for the rapid improvement of any progressive society. Education refines sensitivities and perceptions that contribute to scientific temper, independence of mind and achievements. It is through education of its children, that a nation transmits heritage, recreates its culture, strengthens its economy and ensures its values. Hence, it is right to consider that education is the potential instrument for human resource development.

Cognizing this aspect desirably, Article 45 of the Constitution aims at education to all children of the country. A variety of new challenges made it imperative to evolve new design for education and new policy directions in the context of contemporary realities and future concerns and hence the emergence of the National Policy on Education (NPE, 1986).

The National Policy envisages not only access to all children in the primary schools but also their success. This success has been further delineated as the Minimum Levels of Learning (MLL). In the National budget, increasing allocations are being made for primary education. Primary schools are now available to about 95 per cent of the population with one kilometer of walking distance. There has been considerable increase in the number of qualified and trained teachers. As a result, one notices considerable improvement in the educational situation of the child. However, the country is still far from the goal of Universalisation of Elementary Education (Srivastava, 1995).

The main reason attributed for the inability to achieve the goal of Universalisation of Elementary Education (UEE) is the poor retention capacity of children in the education system. Kaul (1996) lamenting over the existing situation states that there are schools in which no more than 50 of every 100 children who enroll in class I stay on till class V and there are millions of other children who do not get even a fleeting benefit of this dubious dispensation. A study quoted by Misra (1996) reveals that "an estimated 35 per cent of children who enroll in the first grade drop out before completing their primary education, the rate being higher among girls than boys". The large number of early drop outs cancels all the successes that might have been achieved in bringing the child to school.

On account of the poor nature of infrastructure, the National Policy on Education (1986) initiated the Scheme "Operation Blackboard", under which all the primary schools in the country were to be given minimal basic infrastructure in a phased manner. It is also hoped that under the Revised National Education Policy Formulation (1992), substantial improvement in the educational quality will contribute to improving the educational situation of children. One of the most significant contributions of the 20th century, which shall be remembered in History, would then be the global upsurge for "Universalisation of Elementary Education" (Ismail, 1996).

In India, Tamil Nadu took the pioneering step in announcing a legislation to provide compulsory enrolment and retention of children in primary schools with the focus on 6-12 year old (Swaminathan, 1994). Among the important life experience of a growing child, school experiences play a very crucial role, as learning starts with primary education.

The school has the unique responsibility of transmitting knowledge and skills, develop abilities and attitudes with an environment specifically created to aid in the learning process of an individual. However, success during this process depends to a great extent, on the type of schooling provided for the child. It is evident through studies that the measured learning abilities such as productive thinking, reasoning and planning capacity influence academic performance. Therefore, higher the learning abilities, the greater will be the academic achievement.

Academic failure, learning inefficiency, anxiety barriers, dismissals, expulsions, drop outs, reading retardation and a host of other problems are rampant on the educational scene and the percentage of students failing are on the increase. Among them may be the group of learning disabled children, who perform particularly poorly at school despite having otherwise average of above average levels of intellectual ability (Lewis et, al., 1994; Murthy, 1995 and Ahuja, 1996).

The National Joint Committee for Learning Disabilities (NJCLD, 1981) defines learning disabilities as a generic term that refers to heterogeneous group of disorders manifested by significant difficulties in the acquisition and use of listening, speaking, reading, writing, reasoning or mathematical abilities. Even though learning disability may occur concomitantly with other handicapping conditions (e.g. Cultural differences, insufficient / inappropriate instruction, psychogenic factors) it is not the direct result of these conditions or influences.

Sharma (1993) reports that one in ten school going children are learning disabled. These children have an educationally significant discrepancy between estimated intellectual potential and actual level of performance related to basic disorders in the learning processes. Specific types of learning disabilities include dysgraphia (writing disability), dyslexia (reading disability) and dyscalculia (arithmetic disability).

Children with learning disability may not be able to recognize numbers, or big letters from small, may read 12 for 21 for 10, 6 for 9, saw for was, peak for keep, are slow, confused and hesitate to read, miss lines in text, has difficulty in differentiating right from left and in identifying number values in units, tens, hundreds etc.

Research on learning disabilities is in its infancy in India. Even a cursory estimate of this drawback depicts the magnitude of negligence to which such children are exposed. In the absence of proper diagnosis and remedy, most of these children go unnoticed in the guise of low achievers.

The United Nations Declaration of 1981 as "The International Year of the Disabled", and Economic and Social Commission for the Asian and Pacific Region (ESCAP) Declaration of the Decade 1993-2002 as "The Asian and Pacific Decade for the Disabled", request member countries to ensure full equality to those with disabilities along with others, no doubt this has caught the world's attention (Venketaraman, 1995).

Education For All (EFA) including all children with learning disabilities and handicaps as well, by the year 2000 is a global target before the world community. The Universalisation of Elementary Education is planned to be achieved by the end of the first quarter of the 21th century. The task is a challenging one as all children including the disabled have to be educated. This demands that teachers are professionally trained to cater to their specific requirements. Unfortunately, there is little awareness of these aspects in our schools and training institutions. Many children suffer due to lack of awareness on the part of the teachers and parents on disabilities.

Disabilities in reading and writing are often accompanied by disabilities in mathematics. During the first 20 years in the field of learning disabilities, there was little focus on problems with arithmetic computation and the learning of mathematical concepts. More recently however, there has been increased emphasis on these areas.

"Dyscalculia" is the most widely used term for disabilities in mathematics. In general, "Dyscalculia", means inability to calculate. Sometimes the term "Acalculia", is used to refer to complete inability to use mathematical symbols and perform arithmetic computations. The term 'dyscalculia', is reserved for less severe problems in these areas.

Radhakrishnan (1996) considers arithmetic a universal language enabling people to think, record and communicate the elements and relationships involving quantity. It includes both verbal and written symbols that denote size, order, relationship, space, form, distance and time. Mercer and Miller (1992) observed that many students with learning problems have deficiencies in mathematics that result in practical and emotional problems.

The areas of arithmetics and mathematics include the skill and knowledge used in computing answers to written problems and a great deal more. Understanding many concepts and acquiring familiar skills such as managing money, telling time and measuring volume are included in arithmetics. Primary classes being very crucial for children, it is very important that a child develops interest in learning during this period (Ramachandran, 1996).

Researchers estimate that 5-15 per cent of children aged 3 - 15 years are as a group at high risk with social handicap and mental health problems (Mary, 1995). An important study of the National Council for Educational Research and Training (NCERT, 1995) covering 23 states and over 60,000 students expresses concern over the declining learning levels in primary schools and it has been found that the achievements of students in arithmetic and language in class

V are lower than in class IV.

Students with learning disabilities receive their instructiion in general education classrooms. Many students do not have the ability to keep pace with the curriculum, the way it is structured and thereby experience a different kind of segregation, the exclusion from the basic right of education (Schumn et al., 1995). These students are perceived as being lazy, dull, mischievous and notorious in class. Rightly named as "hidden handicap", these children do not get attention or even consideration for the disability, as it is not conspicuous like other disabilities involving sensory, motor or intellectual aspects. Thus, learning disabled children have remained undetected in the present educational system where automatic promotion exists (Menon, 1994).

The problem of learning disability cannot be dealt with medically, it needs to be urgently addressed only through educational remediation. Therefore, early detection of learning disabled children and their remedy is vital at the primary school level. The earlier the remediation, the lesser the damage and the greater the dividend (Mathew, 1996). Rush and Vitale (1994) also favour early prevention stating that the earlier years are the most crucial and if the battle of essential skills in not won before the fifth grade a student can automatically be identified as at risk for school failure.

If children were given activities of their choice, they would learn several things without the help of a teacher. This requires some imagination and planning by the teachers aiming towards a better teaching learning process (Ghose, 1996). The broad view of education requires a shift from the traditional lecture to active student-centered, self-paced, self-discovery methods of learning. This shift requires a commitment to innovation and ability and opportunity to bring about change (Falchikov, 1993).

The National Policy on Education (1986) lays special emphasis on child centered approach, play way and activity based learning in place of formal methods of teaching (Ganesan, 1995). The major focus therefore, should be to enable the teachers to develop proper insight with regard to the nature of learning disability, procedures to identify and diagnose the same and provision of remedial help to the learning disabled children in regular classroom (Jaya and Geetha, 1994).

As the current trend in education of the disabled children is geared towards inclusion, it is ideal to keep the children with scholastic backwardness in regular schools and equip the regular class teachers to identify the child's specific problem in learning. This would in turn lead to helping the child in correcting the problem without labeling him with a diagnostic tag. When "Education for All" is the United Nation's Declaration to be achieved by 2000 AD, such preparation of regular primary teachers is a major milestone towards achieving the goal. The need of the hour is to develop and introduce remediation methods as a special support system to be practiced by teachers to bring about effective responses among children with learning difficulties in mathematics.

Against this backdrop, the investigator designed this study on **"Efficacy of Remedial Package in Augmenting Primary School Teachers' Skills to Help Dyscalculic Children"**, with the following objectives :

(A) Sensitize primary school teachers towards children with learning disabilities
(B) Assess the academic performance of primary school children and identify dyscalculic children among the scholastically backward
(C) Evolve and implement a remedial intervention programme for dyscalculic children and

As higher education becomes competitive, children with this 'hidden handicap' get nowhere into the educational stream and receive no attention to their 'hidden talent'. It is, therefore, envisaged that combined efforts of regular teachers and the parents along with persistent, well motivated approach of the student under the guidance of the remedial teacher would alone bring about a dramatic change in the existing difficulties of the learning disabled.

Research Questions

The study is aimed at answering the following research questions :

(i) What percentage of children exhibit general backwardness in academic subjects?
(ii) What is the proportion of children exhibiting difficulties in mathematics?
(iii) What percentage of children with learning difficulties in mathematics manifest behaviour problems and neuropsychological difficulties?
(iv) What are the outcomes of remedial intervention on selected dyscalculic children?

Operational Definitions

1. Learning disabled

Any average or above average, intelligent child having academic performance below the norm (determined by a standardized measure of academic achievement) and displays substantially greater number of error responses in academic subjects than their peers.

2. 'Dyscalculia'

Mathematical disability referred to as dyscalculia is concerned with specific arithmetic computational deficits faced by children in addition, subtraction, multiplication and division or to specific deficits related to concepts such as spatial relation, shape and size discrimination, one to one correspondence and problem solving.

2

Learning Disability - Basic Concepts

Teachers so called 'Lazy', 'Inattentive', 'Trouble' or 'Stupid' children can be the children with learning disabilities. Any average or above average child having academic performance below the norm can be labelled as learning disabled.

Learning disability refers to retardation, disorder or delayed development in any one or more of the processes of speech, language, reading, spelling, writing or arithmetic. These problems are due to disorder or deficiency in any one or more of basic psychological processes involved in understanding or in using spoken or written language.

A child can be considered learning disabled, if

- he has considerable difficulty in understanding or using spoken language, reading, writing, spelling and / or arithmetic during the developmental period (before 18 years of age)
- he is free from visual, hearing or motor disability, mental retardation, severe emotional problems and
- he has adequate facilities, interest and motivation to learn.

Generally a child with learning disability will have problems with most types of subject matter, while a child with specific learning disability will have major problem with one type of subject material and not with all forms of learning, like with reading (Dyslexia), writing (Dysgraphia) or arithmetic (Dyscalculia).

A learning disabled child may manifest most or some of the following characteristics as reported by specialists in the field:

- **Hyperactivity** : Hyperactive children engage in excessive motor activity that is usually purposeless. They are easily distracted, restless, clumsy, irritable and have short attention span
- **Distractability**: Children with distractability cannot concentrate fully on a specific activity. Irrelevant and inappropriate stimuli become over powering

- **Impulsivity**: An impulsive child talks or acts quickly without considering the consequences
- **Disruptive behaviour**: Disruptive behaviour of aggressive nature towards a victim is common among learning disabled children. Temper tantrums and use of inappropriate language is also commonly found
- **Social withdrawal**: Social withdrawal due to previous failures is common
- **Dependency** : Many of these children exhibit over dependence on parents, teachers and others by requiring excessive help, reassurance and assistance in various activities
- **Perservation**: Children repeat a behaviour long after the response is appropriate. They have difficulty in switching over from one activity to other
- **Poor self-concept** : Frustrated with their learning difficulties, most of these children act disruptively and acquire negative feelings of self-concept
- **Social imperception** : Inability to pickup other's facial expressions, hand and arm gestures, posture, tone of voice or general moods is also common among them
- **Reading difficulties**: The child's reading achievement is significantly lower than what would normally be expected
- **Written difficulties**: The child may exhibit serious problems in written expression and spelling
- **Mathematical difficulties**: The child may find difficulty in basic arithmetic skills, quantitative thinking ability, or any other related mathematic skill
- **Inability to follow directions** : The child may be unable to follow simple oral directions, especially when they are given for the first time
- **Faulty work habits**: The child may organise work poorly, work slowly, frequently confuse directions, or rush through work carelessly
- **Drastic changes in mood**: The child's mood varies from hour to hour without obvious reason.

3

Making Mathematics Teaching Simple

Specific learning disabilities call for focussed instruction and guidance. One of the prominent learning disability relates to mathematics that is inevitably needed in everyday life. Teachers play a key role in teaching mathematics to suit the development level and comprehensive ability of the children.

Children at all levels in the primary school seem to present a wide range of number abilities and interests. In a typical class one may find children who have a sizable amount of mathematical knowledge and readiness for new tasks. Others in the same class have a vague, inaccurate mathematical background and a lack of ability to make normal progress.

Children today are no longer merely trying to memorize symbols, they are learning at a very early age the meaning of numbers by making practical use of available resources at their home and school situations and learning to think quantitatively. Mathematics has come to have such an important place in our modern life that children need to understand it as a means for effective living.

READINESS FOR NUMBER INSTRUCTION

Readiness in mathematics, like readiness in any other fundamental learning process means that the child is ready to learn a new concept with meaning. It is now recognized that readiness in mathematics is a function not only of mental maturity and innergrowth but also of previous experiences, methods of learning, interests, attitude and purposes.

PIAGET (1965) describes several concepts basic to understanding numbers:

(a) Classification

It is the process of understanding relationship such as likeness and differences - classifying objects according to colour, size, shape, function and so on.

Eg : a set of buttons / grouped according to colour, shape, size, etc.

(b) Ordering and seriation

This is important for sequencing numbers. The teacher might display objects in a certain order and ask the child to arrange identical objects in the same order, or sequencing straws by length. Seriation involves ordering items on the basis of change in a property such as length, size or colour.

Eg: teacher places small buttons in a tray one at a time and child places the same number of large buttons in the same manner. The concept is - does each tray have the same number of buttons ?

(c) Conservation

Conservation means that the quantity of an object or the number of objects in a set remains constant regardless of partial rearrangement.

Eg : pouring known volume of water into a tall thin tumbler and a low wide tumbler.

Readiness for facts and concepts - at a higher level

Once formal arithmetic instruction begins, the students must master operations and basic established principles. Operations include addition, subtraction, multiplication and division. Basic principles are less familiar. Alley and Deshler (1979) list the principles important for the learning of mathematics.

(a) **Commutative property of addition** : No matter what order the same numbers are combined in, the sum remains constant

$$a + b = b + a$$
$$3 + 4 = 4 + 3$$

(b) **Commutative property of multiplication** : Regardless of the order of the numbers being multiplied, the product remains constant :

$$a \times b = b \times a$$
$$5 \times 4 = 4 \times 5$$

(c) **Associative property of addition and multiplication**: Regardless of grouping arrangements, the sum or product is unchanged :

Addition :

$$(a + b) + c = a + (b + c)$$
$$(4 + 3) + 2 = 4 + (3 + 2)$$

Multiplication :

$$(a \times b) \times c = a \times (b \times c)$$
$$(5 \times 4) \times 3 = 5 \times (4 \times 3)$$

(d) **Distributive property of multiplication over addition** : This rule relates the two operations

$$a\,(b+c) = (a \times b) + (a \times c)$$
$$5\,(4+3) = (5 \times 4) + (5 \times 3)$$

(e) **Inverse operations** : These principles relate to operations that are opposite in their effects. The following equations demonstrate inverse operations :

Addition and subtraction :

$a + b = c$	$5 + 4 = 9$
$c - a = b$	$9 - 5 = 4$
$c - b = a$	$9 - 4 = 5$

Multiplication and division :

$a \times b = c$	$9 \times 3 = 27$
$c \div a = b$	$27 \div 9 = 3$
$c \div b = a$	$27 \div 3 = 9$

These several concepts help in basic understanding of numerical computations.

Learning Difficulties in Mathematics - Common Errors

It is quite common to observe children with difficulties in mathematics-to forget number facts, have difficulty in figuring out symbols and equations or rules in problem solving. They easily become overwhelmed by a number of problems on a page. It is also seen that these children do their sums in a rote fashion rather than recognize the many possible approaches leading to the same outcome. At times, the children may have difficulty understanding questions that are arranged horizontally rather than vertically.

Table I below illustrates briefly some of the difficulties experienced by children in mathematics.

Table I. Common Learning Difficulties in Mathematics

Conceptual areas	*Learning difficulty*
Perceptual	
Figure-ground	- frequently loses place on worksheet
	- may not finish problems on page
	- reading multi-digit number

	- differentiating between numbers (e.g., 6, 9; 2, 5; or 17, 71) - coins
	- operation symbols
	- copying shapes or problems
	- writing across paper in a straight line
Discrimination	- before-after; problems with Compu-tations involving up-down (eg., addition), left - right (regroup-ing); problems aligning numbers in multipli-cation and division
Spatial	- putting decimals in right place
	- spacing manipulatives into patterns
	- using number line
	- understanding numbers (directional)
Memory	
Short-term	- retaining facts
	- remembering all the steps in an algorithm
	- retaining meaning of symbols
Long-term	- difficulty mastering facts over time
	- initial difficulty with problems during revision
	- forgets steps in algorithm
Sequential	- counting rationally
	- completing all steps in a multi-step computation problem
	- solving multi-step word problems
Language	
Receptive	- relating arithmetic terms to meaning (e.g.,minus, add, divide, regroup, multiply, place value) words that have multiple meanings (e.g., carry over)
Expressive	- the vocabulary of arithmetic
	- oral drills in arithmetic
	- verbalizing steps in solving a word problem
Behavioural pattern	
Impulsive	- makes careless mistakes in computation
	- responds incorrectly and rapidly in oral drills
	- attending to detail in solving problems
	- completing work in assigned time, start a problem and not finish it
Short attention	- goes on to next problem, may frequently be off-task
	- switching from one operation to another
Perservation	- may work very slowly and go over work several times
	- oral drills
	- oral work problems
	- counting on from within a sequence

Auditory	- writing numbers on dictation
	- hearing number patterns

Difficulties of Students with Learning Disabilities Affecting Mathematics Performance

Learning difficulty	*Problems*
Reading	- Understanding the vocabulary of problems
Reasoning	- word problems
	- comparisons of size, quantity
	- use of symbols (e.g. >, <, ×, = 1)
	- applying abstract level of mathematical concepts and operations
Motor	- writing numbers legibly, with speed and accuracy
	- writing numbers in small spaces (i.e., writes large)

Common errors

Lack of competence in the four computational skills-addition, subtraction, multiplication, division account for 90 per cent of the difficulty experienced among children. In order to be more functional in these skill areas learning disabled students need a great deal of rehearsal and repetition to énsure that these skills become internalized and errors commonly made are virtually reduced. Below is a list of common arithmetic errors with a brief analysis along with a checklist for teachers and parents to identify the types of errors made in the four basic skill areas. (Table II).

Table II. Common Arithmetic Errors

Sl. No.	*Analysis*	*Example*
1.	Lacks mastery of basic facts (a) Addition	32 + 43 7④
	(b) Multiplication	32 × 3 ⑧6
2.	Subtracts incorrectly within the division algorith	73 3)230 - 21 ①0 - 9 1

Sl. No.	Analysis	Example
3.	Does not complete addition (a) Does not write whole number	85 + 43 1 28
	(b) Leaves out numbers in vertical addition	4 8 2 + 3 15
4.	Rewrites a numeral without computing	72 +①5 77 --- >32 × 3 ③6
5.	Does not complete subtraction	7) 397 (4 ---> 28
6.	Does not complete division because of incomplete subtraction	7) 397 (4 -280 ①7
7.	Fails to complete division; stops at first partial quotient	7) 370 (5 - 35 20
8.	Fails to complete division; leaves remainder equal to or greater than divisor.	9) 729 (80 72 90
9.	Confuses role of zero in subtraction with role of zero in multiplication	37 -20 10
10.	Subtracts top digit from bottom digit whenever regrouping is involved	30 18 28
11.	Confuses role of zero in multiplication with multiplicative identity	7 × 0 = 7
12.	Lacks skills with addition algorithm : (a) Adds units to units and tens :	37 + 2 59
	(b) adds units to tens and hundreds:	342 +36 678

Sl. No.	Analysis	Example
	(c) Adds unit to tens and hundreds	132 +6 798
	(d) Is unable to add horizontally: 345+7+13 = 185 Think : 3+7+1 = 11; writes 1 4+3 = 7 (+1 carried) 5 = 5 May add zero or one to make sum greater	8 5 ①85
13.	Does not regroup units to tens	37 +25 5②
14.	When there are fewer digits in subtraction : (a) subtract unit from all unit and from tens (and hundreds) : (b). subtracts tens from tens and hundreds	783 -2 ⑤⑥1 783 -23 560
15.	Does not rename tens digit after regrouping	54 -9 ⑤5
16.	When two zeroes are involved, renames hundreds twice but does not rename tens	700 -326 284
17.	Decrease hundreds digit by one when not necessary	371 -134 ①37
18.	Adds regrouped number to tens but does not multiply * 7 × 5 = 35; 30 +30 = 60	35 × 7 65 *
19.	Multiplies by only one number	457 × 12 914
20.	"Carries" wrong number	⑧ 67 × 40 3220
21.	Does not regroup; treats each column as separate addition example	23 +8 211
22.	Subtracts smaller digit from larger at all times to avoid remainder	273 -639 446

ERROR ANALYSIS CHECKLIST IN ADDITION, SUBTRACTION, MULTIPLICATION AND DIVISION

Addition

Error in combinations
Counting
Adds carried number last
Forgets to add carried number
Repeats work, partly done
Adds carried number irregularly
Writes number to be carried
Irregular procedure in column
Carries wrong number
Groups two or more numbers
Split numbers into parts
Use wrong fundamental operation
Loses place in column
Depends on visualization
Disregards column position
Errors in reading numbers
Drops one or more tens
Derives unknown combination from familiar one
Disregards one column
Error in writing the answer
Carrying, with nothing to carry
Adds in pairs
Add same digit in two columns
Writes carried number in answer
Adds same number twice
Omits one or more digits

Subtraction

Errors in combinations
Does not allow for having borrowed
Errors due to zero
Say example backwards
Fails to borrow; give zero as answer
Adds instead of subtraction
Errors in reading
Use same digits in two columns
Derive unknown from known combinations
Omit a column
Split numbers
Borrow when not necessary
Ignore a digit
Error due to digits being same
Use minuend as remainder
Reverse digits in remainder
Skip one or more details
Increase digit after borrowing
Base subtraction on multiplication combination
Use trial and error addition

Multiplication

Errors in combinations
Error in adding the carried number
Write rows of zeros
Carry a wrong number
Errors in addition
Forgets to carry
Error in single zero combinations, zero as multiplier
Errors due to zero in multiplier
Use wrong process
Errors in reading numbers
Omit digit in product
Error in writing product
Error in carrying a zero
Omit digit in multiplier
Error due to zero in multiplicand
Illegible figures
Forgets to add partial products
Split multiplier

Error in single zero combinations, zero as multiplier	Multiply by same digit twice
Confuse product when multiplier has two or more digits	Reverse digits in product
Multiply by adding	Write the tables wrong
	Misses a digit

Division

Errors in division combinations	Group too many digits in dividend
Errors in subtraction	Error in reading
Errors in multiplication	Use dividend or divisor as quotient
Use remainder larger than divisor	Found quotient by adding
Found quotient by trial multiplication	Reverse divided and divisor
Neglect to use remainder	Use digits of divisor separately
Omits zero	Write all remainders at end of problem
Counts to get quotient	Misinterprets table
Repeat part of multiplication table	Use digit in dividend twice
Use short division form for long division	Use second digit of divisor to
Write remainders within problem	Begin dividing at units digit of dividend
Omit zero resulting from zero	
Omit final remainder	
Use long division form for short division	

Developing Computational Skills

There is something for everybody to gain from the "Universal Language", that is mathematics, the earlier a child is initiated to this 'world of order', the easier it would be for the child to imbibe the quality that the discipline symbolises.

While students with learning disabilities are usually first identified because of their reading problems, the correlation between reading and mathematics is high for many students. Both are languages. One primarily qualitative, the other quantitative. Mathematics demands the same essential features - knowledge of basic skills, conceptual understanding and speed. Learning disabled students may have problems in one, two or three of these elements.

It has been estimated that lack of competence in the four computational skills (addition, subtraction, multiplication, division) account for 90 per cent of the difficulty experienced by adults in everyday life. In order to be functional in these skills, students need a great deal of rehearsal, repetition, over-teaching and over-learning to ensure that these skills become internalized and come automatically to the student as needed. Learning these basic skills often become monotonous, it is important to include games, concrete and abstract materials, multisensory approaches and problems the students themselves bring to the learning situation. Most of the mathematical programs indicate an appropriate sequence that the teacher can follow. It is important, however, to discover at what point the student is having difficulty.

Counting is a necessary skill beginning for addition and multiplication. Counting by 1's, 2's, 5's and 10's underly addition facts. Adding doubles (8+8) is easier and faster than adding different numbers. Therefore, teaching students to manipulate numbers into doubles improves their accuracy and speed. Another important conversion is in any problem where a number can be converted to 10. Examples of this is changing 9 + 6 to 10 + 5. A third conversion involves position. Students need to understand that 2 + 6 is the same as 6 + 2 and that it is more efficient to count on to the bigger number i.e., 6, 7, 8, rather than 2, 3, 4, 5, 6, 7, 8.

Multiplication is even more dependent on counting than is addition. When students understand the relationship between counting and multiplication, their ability to quickly answer problems that involve these facts is improved. The following matrix involving zero to ten in counting and multiplication, increases the student's, understanding of numbers and makes them less dependent on rote learning.

If multiplication is a problems for students, have them build this matrix beginning with the counting they already have mastered. This usually involves 1's, 2's, 3's, 5's and 10's. Next, teach them to count by 4's. Many students use their fingers while they count. In fact, it is useful for them to realise that using fingers can be quite appropriate. However, eventully they should discover that the problem with fingers is that they are slow.

Multiplication Chart

1	2	3	4	5	6	7	8	9	10	11	12
2	4	6	8	10	12	14	16	18	20	22	24
3	6	9	12	15	18	21	24	27	30	33	36
4	8	12	16	20	24	28	32	36	40	44	48
5	10	15	20	25	30	35	40	45	50	55	60
6	12	18	24	30	36	42	48	54	60	66	72
7	14	21	28	35	42	49	56	63	70	77	84
8	16	24	32	40	48	56	64	72	80	88	96
9	18	27	36	45	54	63	72	81	90	99	108
10	20	30	40	50	60	70	80	90	100	110	120
11	22	33	44	55	66	77	88	99	110	121	132
12	24	36	48	60	72	84	96	108	120	132	144

Matrix Showing Relationship Between Counting and Multiplication

	0	1	2	3	4	5	6	7	8	9	10
0	0	0	0	0	0	0	0	0	0	0	0
1	0	1	2	3	4	5	6	7	8	9	10
2	0	2	4	6	8	10	12	14	16	18	20
3	0	3	6	9	12	15	18	21	24	27	30
4	0	4	8	12	16	20	24	28	32	36	40
5	0	5	10	15	20	25	30	35	40	45	50
6	0	6	12	18	24	30	36	42	48	54	60
7	0	7	14	21	28	35	42	49	56	63	70
8	0	8	16	24	32	40	48	56	64	72	80
9	0	9	18	27	36	45	54	63	72	81	90
10	0	10	20	30	40	50	60	70	80	90	100

Next teach the nine times tables. Many students thinks this is very difficult but in fact, the nine times tables involves many cognitive aspects that help them to learn and remember it easily. Have the student look at the nines table separately to discover some of the relations between the numbers. First have them put down those products they already have inserted into the grid.

Show them that the number in the tens column increases from 0 to 9. While the number in the ones column decreases from 9 to 10. Another approach is to convert the 9 to 10, multiply by 10 and subtract the number to be multiplied.

Nine Times Grid

$9 \times 0 = 0$	
$9 \times 1 = 9$	$0 + 9 = 9$
$9 \times 2 = 18$	$1 + 8 = 9$
$9 \times 3 = 27$	$2 + 7 = 9$
$9 \times 4 = 36$	$3 + 6 = 9$
$9 \times 5 = 45$	$4 + 5 = 9$
$9 \times 6 = 54$	$5 + 4 = 9$
$9 \times 7 = 63$	$6 + 3 = 9$
$9 \times 8 = 72$	$7 + 2 = 9$
$9 \times 9 = 81$	$8 + 1 = 9$
$9 \times 10 = 90$	$9 + 0 = 9$

For example, $9 \times 7 = (10 \times 7) - 7 = 70 - 7 = 63$. Finally the student should always check the answer by adding the two numbers in the product, which should always add up to nine; if it does not, the answer is wrong and the student must do the problem again. This matrix may be pasted on the inside cover of the student's mathematics workbook for easy reference. The matrix can also be used to help LD students understand 'zero' since it is visually apparent that no matter how big the multiplicand is, if the multiplier is 'zero', the answer is 'zero'.

(a) Perceptual problems

Some students mix up the symbols in calculations, i.e., x read as +, - read as ÷, - read as = Flash cards with these symbols prominently drawn and multisensory approaches are two useful approaches.

In assessment, analysis of the errors the student can pinpoint his or her problems. One that is frequently found is subtraction comes from inadequate teaching. A frequent instruction when teaching subtraction is to "Take the small numbers from the big one". While this is true in general, it is not always true when dealing with ones and tens in three digit numbers.

Eg.	831	481
	-465	- 68
	43 ④	42⑦

Helping a student with this problem is essentially reteaching subtraction including place value and borrowing. Thus, multisensory approaches, especially those that include concrete materials that the student can manipulate, are very helpful for students at all ages.

(b) Word problems

Another difficulty the student has with both verbal problem and computations are the cluttered pages. This can be most easily remédiated by reducing the number of questions per page, or by boxing them.

Many students think that mathematics is completely structured with only one method of finding an answer. A creative approach that can help students understand underlying aspects in mathematics involves attending to essential facts in problems and brainstorming a variety of possible solutions.

Mathematical Terms in Basic Computations

Operation		*Terms*
Addition	8	- addend
	+ 4	- add
	12	- sum
Subtraction	9	- minued
(take away)	- 4	- subtract
	5	- difference
Subtraction	19	- sum
(take away)	- 4	- known addend
	5	- missing addend
Multiplication	8	- multiplicand
	× 5	- multiplier
	40	- product
Division	8	- quotient
	6) 49	- dividend
	divisor 48	
	1	- remainder

STRATEGIES AND COMPONENTS FOR EFFECTIVE MATHEMATICS INSTRUCTION

Examining the mathematical deficits of students have resulted in a number of initial teaching and remediation methods incorporating Concrete - Representational - Abstract (CRA) teaching sequence. Implicit in this method is and emphasis on teaching students to understand the concepts of mathematics prior to memorising facts, algorithm and operations. Although the CRA sequence is widely advocated for mathematical learning, it is rarely used in a systematic manner during instruction.

According to the CRA sequence, instruction begins at 'concrete level' where the student uses three dimensional objects to solve computational problems. After successfully solving several problems at the concrete level, the student can proceed to the representational level.

At the representational level, drawings are used to solve computational problems. For example, in solving the problem 7×3, the student is instructed to look at the first number and draw that many groups using circles. Considering the next number 3, draw three tallies in each circles. The student then counts the tallies in the circles 21 to arrive at the answer. After successfully solving several multiplication problems at this level, the student begins to work at the abstract level.

At the abstract level, the student looks at the computation problems and tries to solve it using objects or drawings. The student reads the problems, thinks of a way to compute the answer and writes the answer.

No objects or drawings are used unless the students is not able to answer a problem. Success in mathematics requires the ability to solve problems at the abstract level, therefore it is essential that students achieve mastery at this level.

COMPONENTS OF EFFECTIVE MATHEMATICS INSTRUCTION

The following are some of the components to impart effective mathematics instruction to children with difficulties:

1. Select appropriate mathematics content

Recommending reforms in the content of mathematics curriculum if required.

Answers not only in written work - but improve their ability to think critically and understand concept, operation and real-life applications as important goals of the curriculum.

(a) **Problem solving**
Applying previously acquired information to different situations.
Solving both verbal and non-verbal problems.

(b) **Communicating mathematical ideas**
Students should learn the language and notation of mathematics
Present mathematical ideas using manipulative objects, drawings, in writing and while speaking.

(c) **Applying mathematics to every day situation**
Students may be encouraged to translate daily experience into mathematical representations (i.e., graphs, tables, diagrams, or experiences and interpret the results).

(d) **Focusing on appropriate computational skills**
Gain proficiency in using operations
(addition, subtraction, multiplication, division with whole numbers and decimals)
Knowledge of basic facts is essential along with mental arithmetic skill

2. Establish goal

(a) Setting instructional goals - based on students' learning needs

(b) Students need a challange rather than easy success, set difficult but attainable goal.

3. Provide systematic and explicit instruction

(a) Demonstration - prompt and practise sequence, enhances the student's outcomes.

(b) Explicit instruction is important for facilitating positive academic growth involves highly organised, step by step procedure, identifies the target's, skill presentation

(c) Effective instruction enables students to understand the direction and demands of the task

(d) Systematic use of learning principles in effective instruction
Negative student outcomes occur when attention is not maintained, positive reinforcement is used, spaced and varied practice occurs and motivation is held high.
Efficient teaching process involves-demonstration, guided practice with prompts and independent practice with feedback.

4. Teach students to understand mathematical concepts

The use of Concrete-Representational - Abstract (CRA) sequence, is an excellent way to teach students with learning problems to understand the concepts, operations and applications.

5. Monitor Progress

Involves the teacher frequently checking on the behaviour and academic work of students and making instructional adaptations based on observations. Frequent monitoring is a key to student learning.

6. Provide progress

Academic feedback is positively associated with student learning and is the best among the teacher behaviour for promoting positive learning outcome. Feedback is important in promoting the following student outcomes:

* Mastery of content and skills for further learning
* Ability to study and learn independently
* Plan and monitor learning activities
* Motivation for continued learning
* Confidence in one's ability as a learner

7. Teach to mastery

Mastery learning refers to teaching a skill to a level of automaticity. It provides numerous benefits such as:

* Improved retention and ability to compute higher level problems
* Finishing timed tests
* Receiving higher grades
* Developing positive attitude towards mathematics

8. Teach problem solving

Problem solving should be of top priority in mathematics instruction. It includes : components such as :

* Mathematical knowledge base
* Apply acquired knowledge to new situations
* Actively engage in thinking process

9. Teach generalization

This refers to performance of the targeted behaviour in different, non-training conditions.

Selected instructional practices include :

* Motivation to learn
* Periodic discussions with students
* Variety of examples and experiences
* Skills to mastery level
* Solving problems pertinent to daily living

10. Promote positive attitude towards mathematics

Many students with learning problems have a history of mathematical failures. Attitudes, beliefs and motivation play an important role in the learning of mathematics

According to Mercer and Miller (1992) selected guidelines include

* Setting challenging but attainable goals
* Ensuring success
* Use progress charts to provide feedback
* Communicate positive expectations
* Model or illustrate positive attitude
* Reinforce students for more effort.

4

Principles in Remediation

Lack of competence in the conceptual skill areas (addition, subtraction, multiplication and division) necessitates, learning disabled students to take up great deal of rehearsal, repetition, over teaching and over learning to ensure that these skills become internalised and come automatically to the student as and when needed.

Since learning these skills often become monotonous, it is important to include games, concrete and abstract materials, multisensory approaches to problems the students themselves bring to the learning situation.

The general principles that relate to remediation are enlisted below:

Remediation is a determination of the reasons why a student has been unable or unwilling to tackle a task and is unable to meet behavioural and/or performance expectations. It is an analysis of how the task has been presented and the skills and background knowledge that are required to execute the task effectively. These analysis are the most important aspects of remediation and failure to do any task may have a variety of possible causes. Some of the questions one might ask are:

1. Does the child pay attention to, understand and remember what is expected of him? Does he understand the language communicated?
2. Has he experienced many failures in the past that he is afraid to attempt the task and fail, or to express himself lest he makes an error?
3. Is the task - be it speaking, writing, an academic subject, motor co-ordination, a chore or a social activity - too complex or too overwhelming?
4. Does he have a notion of how long the task will take and how to fit it into his schedule? Does he reprioritize to ensure that

important tasks and commitments are attended to on schedule? Are the tasks completed?

5. Does he have the prerequisite knowledge in doing the task. The child may have unexpected gaps in knowledge. Is he aware of what zero means, of what a symbol represents, or what a formulae stands for ?
6. Does he have the skills to do task such as the co-ordination skills to print or write and the spelling skills?
7. If he is unable to execute the task in the typical fashion, is he aware of alternative possibilities?
8. Does he perceive the patterns such as (2 times 4) = (12 - 4) ?
9. In what kinds of situations and with which groups do the difficulties arise?
10. What usually happens before the problem occurs ?

Simple clues based on principles

To educate a child for mathematical competency and understanding, the curriculum needs to be built upon the following basic principles:

1. **The child needs to discover, understand and master the various mathematical concepts**

For example understanding the concept of number 4 would be indicated by such abilities as knowing that

4 is one more than 3 = 3+1 = 4
4 is one less than 5 = 5-1 = 4
4 is more than 0, 1, 2, 3
4 is less than 5, 6, 7, 8
4 is represented using symbols to represent a set such as 1111 = 4
or
OOOO = 4

Mastering the concept of 4 in addition, subtraction, multiplication, and division is to be provided.

2. **The child needs to discover, understand and master the various mathematical meanings**

For exmple, knowing that 678 is 6 hundred 7 tens and 8 can also be represented as the number in a pocket chart, place value frame and on abacus.

Other aspects include knowing that addition and multiplication are combining actions, whereas subtraction and division are separating actions.

3. **Once the child's understanding of the how and why of arithmetic develops, he needs to work for automatic mastery to become skillful in the use of mathematics**
   This means being able to compute, check results, measure accurately and describe various numerical situations.
4. **Throughout the entire instructional programme the development of problem-solving ability must be carried on**
   Problems give purpose to the arithmetic instruction and are basic to the introduction and application of new concepts, facts and processes. All drill and practice exercises or sequences should involve problem solving.

Following are some of the activities that may be included:

Activity 1: Volume

Aim : Measure the volume of different substances.

Materials required : A glass measuring jar, a ball, stone, potato, egg, tomato, paper, pencil, graph paper.

Method : Put a small ball in the jar and cover it with water. Note the measure of volume of water reached on the jar. Next remove the ball and again note the measure of water. Subtract to find the volume of the ball.

Conclusion : Similarly take the measure for all other collected items. Finally enable the students make a graph of the same.

Activity 2: Size and Weight

Aim : To find out the objects when the weight is the same.

Materials : Scale, weighing balance, measuring jar, china clay.

Method : Create different shapes using the given clay for example, a very flat shape, a cube and slighter flatter one and finally make a note of the weight of the same.

Conclusion : The shapes thus made can then be put in a jar of water to measure the volume of the same.

Activity 3: Weight

Aim : To make a guess of which is heavier by just looking at the object.

Materials : Balance, rice, dhal, sand, salt, popcorn, groundnuts, chalk, etc.

Method : Take equal measurements of all the items mentioned above and weigh them. Check with the guess made.
The weight of one's own classmates 10 of them can also be made in making a guess of who is heavier.

Conclusion : Helps in knowing the approximate weight of the various substances used daily in the household or in the class room.

Activity 4: Measurement of length and height

Aim : Measuring length of arms and height of students

Materials : Measuring tape, paper, pencil

Method : Initially help the students measure the length of the arm of 10 students in the class. Next measure their height using the same measuring tape standing against a wall if there is no proper measuring

Conclusion : Enables gain in knowledge on approximate length and breadth of various items and students height.

Manipulative Aids and Resources

The earlier the people are made to realise that mathematics is the king of all arts and queen of all science and the earlier mathematics is considered and accepted as a creative subject of higher applicability, the better will be the quality of individual and social life.

Remediation cannot happen successfully without ample resource materials. Following pages project innumerable activities that could be conducted for experiential learning. Mathematical concepts come alive with clearly marked simple directions, appealing illustrations and a variety of self-motivating exercises. Working with well-graded worksheets at home or in school helps children to develop skills and to build confidence. Young children will love these exercises which instill the idea that learning is exciting, rewarding and fun.

While this series provides enough opportunity for gaining

computational skill, no effort has been spared to help the child develop the faculty of thinking and reasoning.

Use of manipulative aids

- Prior to abstract experiences, instruction must proceed from concrete (manipulative) experiences to semi-concrete experiences
- Manipulative aids help students understand and develop images of mathematical processes
- The activity must accurately represent the actual process. For example, a direct correlation should exist between the manipulative activities and the paper-pencil activities
- More than one manipulative object should be used in teaching a concept
- The aid should be used individually by each student
- Manipulative experience must involve the moving of objects as learning occurs from the student's physical action on the objects, and not from the objects.

The teacher can use a variety of resources/indigenous materials available in the environment to facilitate learning of mathematical concepts among children.

PLAY MATERIALS/RESOURCES FOR TEACHING MATHEMATICAL SKILLS

Listed below are some of the resource materials which have proved to be beneficial in developing mathematics skills among children.

Date calendar, paper cups, tooth picks, tamarind seeds, ice cream cups and spoons, batteries, rexin - shape bits, clock representation, buttons in different colours/shapes, pictures of cycles/bikes/cars chocolates/doll, etc., bottle caps, items that float/sink, measuring tapes, paper plates, paper napkins/ribbons, plastic spoons, containers with lids, marbles, small boxes, artificial flowers, balls of different sizes, advertisements-cycles/bikes/cars/chocolates/dolls, etc., cassettes, bamboo, drinking straws, coloured chalk, stones, pebbles, ribbons and clothes and cloths clip.

Games

Games for Mathematical Concept Learning

Games which are and integral part of play, constitute an

invaluable component of education in childhood. Games provide movement, exercise concept learning and are also a form of recreation in addition to providing innumerable benefits to children.

Since play has emerged as a strategy to promote harmonious and holistic development of children, games can also contribute towards conceptual learning of mathematics.

Title of the game : **GO HUNTING**
Materials required : A bowl, large number of buttons, pebbles
Category : Individual

Procedure: Have large number of buttons/pebbles ready in a box. When its time to start the game, scatter all the button/pebbles on the floor. Tell the children that they have five minutes to collect as many pebbles/buttons as they can. Ask them to scramble for the buttons/pebbles. When the time is up, enable the children add the buttons/pebbles collected by each one. The child who has collected the maximum number of pebbles/buttons, is the winner.

****

Title of the game : **THREAD BEADS**
Materials required : Large/beads/buttons, thread
Category : Individual

Procedure: Give each child ten or more beads/buttons and a similar length of thread. The child who threads all the beads/buttons first and tells the total number is the winner. He/she receive applause from the classmates.

****

Title of the game : **COLLECT MARBLES**
Materials required : Chalk piece, marbles/pebbles/any one choosen
Category : Individual

Procedure: A circle (about 30 cm wide) is drawn on the floor. All children stand in a circle. Each child is given 1-2 marbles. 15-20 marbles are kept in the centre. A small circle is drawn around the marbles. Each child using the marbles given to her/him tries to displace the marble from the circle in the centre. The objects thus brought out of the circle is/are kept by the child. The child who is not able to knock of any marble from the circle, in the centre, has to keep her/his marble in the centre. The child who has collected maximum number of marbles, is the winner.

Title of the game : **GROUP THE DOTS**
Materials required : Cardboard pieces, coloured paper
Category : Team

Procedure: Cut the cardboard into equal number of circles, triangles, squares, diamonds and rectangles, stick, colour paper on the pieces and provide each team with equal number and the same type of pieces. Mark one dot on some pieces, two dots on some pieces, three on some, four on some and five and so on. Make sure that there are equal number of pieces of each type (i.e., equal number of one dot pieces, two dots etc.) for each team

****

Title of the game : **GUESS THE NUMBER**
Materials required : Small twigs/sticks/bamboo
Category : Group game
Area : Indoor or outdoor

Procedure: Each child is given five small twigs/bamboo. All are made to it in a circle. They will then transfer some or all of the five twigs into one hand, unseen by others. The children then start guessing the total number of twigs. The child whose guess is closest or equal to the number of the total twigs is the winner.

Rules of the game :
* Each student is given only five twigs/sticks
* All children must keep their palms closed till the last child guesses the number
* Numbers once said should not be repeated

****

Title of the game : **MONEY VALUE**
Materials required : Coins of one rupee, two and five
Category : Indoor/outdoor

Description of the game : Each team is given four coins which is distributed in the team. Instructions are given by the teacher which should be followed. For example, add five, multiply ten, add two subtract fifty. The team finishing first is the winner.

Rules of the game :
* Calculation may be done on paper
* There should be no confusion
* Each child gets a coin each
* Teacher's decision is considered final

5

Remedial Intervention Strategies

Intervention strategies that can be used in remedial intervention are detailed below:

Remedial intervention for dyscalculic children

Mathematical concept	*Manipulative resource*	*Activity*
(A) Classification		
1. Sorting		
(a) Give students objects that differ in one at tribute e.g., colour.	Coloured chalks, beads straw	Sort the given chalks by colour and put them in the tray
(b) At advanced level, in crease the complexity of the classification in any 2 or 3 qualities/ attributes.	Buttons, drinking straws, ribbons	Sort the given buttons by size shape and colour
2. Matching and sorting		
The first step in the development of num ber concept is the ability to focus on and recognize a single object or shape	A collection of assorted objects, beads, blocks, seeds, pulses, nuts	Choose only objects of round shape
3. Recognition of groups		
Develop competency in the above concepts	Assorted objects to enable grouping	Pile together objects that can be grouped to your choice

Mathematical concept	*Manipulative resource*	*Activity*
4. Number stamp		
Make a set of numerals with matching dots using	Paint colours, at the end of a pencil or chalk	*Students asked to make matching dots colours for the numbers written on cards
(B) Ordering		
1. Serial order and relationships		*State the number Before 6 After 8
Concept- Before	Pebbles, shells	In between 9-15
After	leaves, flowers	
Inbetween	petals, seeds	
Seriation- First		Size- big, small
Second		Weight - heavy, -light
Third	Flowers, stones	
Last	chalks, dolls	
Order by size, colour, weight, volume	Glass of water or sand	Volume - indicate more-less on measuring known volume of water or sand
2. Many lines with chalk offered and exercises provided to develop number concepts	Draw chalk lines indicating *1 2 3 4 5 6 *10 20 30 40 50 60 a line of blocks * 100 200 300 400 500 600 a line in sand	*Number lines when touched, walked upon or jumped upon provides a helpful understanding in using symbols, numerals and their relationships
3. Pattern games Opportunities are provided to discover patterns selecting the objects in a series	Colour symbols, cut outs of shapes, numberals from calendars provided	Develop patterns using different colours
4. Relationship between concept of soze and length compare and contrast between sizes, shapes provided	Thermocol shapes, trees chalks, (big/small), clips, clothes clips, screws, nails, buttons.	* Compare objects on paper in terms of shape, size, colour, texture and purpose

Mathematical concept	*Manipulative resource*	*Activity*
(C) One To One Correspondence		
1. Pairing		
This provides a foundation for counting by matching one object with another	Pairing objects in the kitchen e.g. spoons, forks, tumblers, plates Setting a dining table	* Arrange a row of spoons, ask the student to match spoons with the prearranged row. Provide this experience of setting the dining table
2. Counting		
Provide motor activities for counting.	Observing at any visual or auditory stiumali, provided	Stringing beads and counting the total number by colour shape and size.
	Listening, pointing to objects, skipping objects, counting in 2's, 3's, 4's and 5's using ice cream cups, spoons, bamboo, sticks as indicated.	Placing objects in required numbers. Print numbers on cups to fill required number of objects.
3. Recognition of numbers		
Recognize the numbers	Objects, cardborard, sand paper	Match the correct printed number with the number of objects or along printed numerals.
Recognize the printed numbers in words	Scale, ruler measuring tape, weighing balance rupees, coins, given to develop * Use color variation for concept development.	Measure height and weight of individual student and write in words. Length of tables, door, windows, blackboard measured.

Problem	*Error*	*Reason*	*Strategy*
(D) Mirror Writing or rotation of numbers			
2 3 5 6 7 9	S ε Z ୧\9 Γ ୧	Lack of concentration Poor identification of numbers Poor pre-writing skills Poor hand writing skills Awkward writing position Difficulty in numerical writing Poor visual orientation perceptual problems	Torch light tracking Writing in air Writing in sand Writing on the back (a) behind one's (neighbours) shoulders (b) on one's hand (c) spread color powders or plain sand-
(E) Reversing digits			
12 16 17 19	21 61 71 91	Poor memory Poor concept of numerals See them reversed Perceptual reading problem Inability to put thought in writing Poor retention of what has been studied for sequencing	Torch light tracking Writing in air Writing in sand Writing on the back (a) behind one's (neighbours) shoulders (b) on one's hand (c) Spread colour powders or plain sand-
Numerals Concrete to abstract method Concept of 5		Poor concept development	 -five  -five

Problem	*Error*	*Reason*	*Strategy*
		Poor oral and writing skill	 -five -five 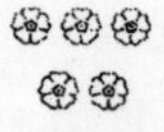 -five
Concept of 8		Poor concept development Poor oral and writing skill	 -Eight  -Eight  -Eight  -Eight
Concept of zero		Poor concept development Poor oral and writing skill Abstract idea	The concept or Zero is taught by counting in the absence or presence of zero Reduce one by one and count 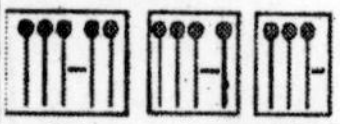 3-2 3-1 3-0
Numerals Addition facts of zero 3 + 0 2 + 0 1 + 0 0 + 0	3 + 0 = 0	Unclear concept	 3+2=5 3+1=4 3+0=3
	1 + 0 = 0	Poor orientation to addition facts	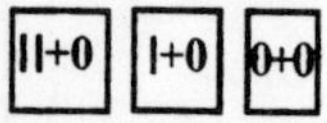 2+0=2 1+0=1 0+0=0
		Problem with zero	✶Take two piles of drinking straws reduce one pile by

Problem	*Error*	*Reason*	*Strategy*
			removing one by one giving the sum each time. ✱ Next remove the straw from the existing pile giving the sum of the counts.
Multiplication facts of zero 4 x 0 2 x 0 3 x 0 2 x 0 1 x 0	4 x 0 = 0 3 x 0=0	Poor concept Poor knowledge of multiplication facts	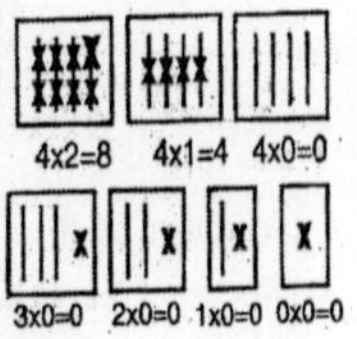 ✱ From the criss cross placement of the pencils/ sticks/straws reduce one pile by removing one by one giving the sum at each stage. ✱✱ In the second stage, remove the vertical pencils/ stick one by one giving the multiplication fact. ✱ This is called the flow technique and the effect of this type of "handson experience" learning inevitably leads

Problem	*Error*	*Reason*	*Strategy*
			to correct solutions
Writing in words			
0	Zour, 0	- Perceptual problem	Using different colours for
12	Twlve	- Grammatical error	different concepts
19	Ninteen	- Poor retantion of what has been studied	Enhancing initial recognition skills
36	Thiraty six	- Inability to put thoughts into writing	Repeated exercise
40	Fourty	- Teandency to omit words	
50	Fivety	- Poor handwriting	
96	Ninty six, Ninty six	- Poor vocabulary skill	
108	Hunder eight	- Deficiency in the ability to learn things in a sequence.	
214	Two hunder fourty, Twenty one hunder one fourty	- Confusion regarding place value	
370	Three hunder seventy, three seventy	- Spelling error	 Using abacus
Place value			
4020 110 40209 724543 43276519	4000020 10010 40201 7245043 432706519	- Disorganisation - Difficulty in understanding place value	(a) In columns and rows

<table>
<tr><th>Problem</th><th>Error</th><th>Reason</th><th>Strategy</th></tr>
<tr><td>615250
21800050
1569852
810960</td><td></td><td>- Serious inability to spell
- Poor orientation
- Poor direction ality
- Movement right to left is difficult to comprehend</td><td><table>
<tr><th>C</th><th>L</th><th>TH</th><th>H</th><th>T</th><th>U</th></tr>
<tr><td></td><td></td><td>4</td><td>0</td><td>2</td><td>0</td></tr>
<tr><td></td><td></td><td></td><td>1</td><td>1</td><td>0</td></tr>
<tr><td></td><td></td><td>40</td><td>2</td><td>0</td><td>1</td></tr>
<tr><td></td><td>7</td><td>24</td><td>5</td><td>4</td><td>3</td></tr>
<tr><td>4</td><td>32</td><td>76</td><td>5</td><td>1</td><td>9</td></tr>
<tr><td></td><td></td><td></td><td></td><td></td><td></td></tr>
</table></td></tr>
<tr><td>Place value (continued)

(a) 75
(b) 105
(c) 165
(d) 1065
(e) 2605
(f) 1288</td><td></td><td>Using bamboo sticks or drinking straws Step 1: using bamboo sticks/ straws to the students
Step 2: Bundles of 10's are to be made

Step 3: To make 70/ seven bundles of 10's are kept aside and for 5-five single sticks are selected to make 75.
Step 4: For 100's bundles of 100's are made and similarly the sum 165 can be made
165 = 100's (1) + 10's (6) +5
= 165 is made
(a) Using abacus
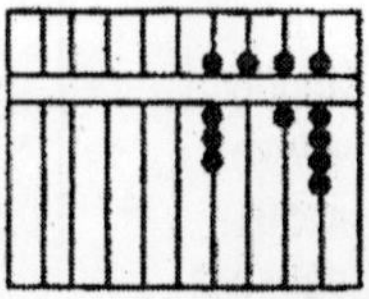
Th HTU</td><td>(b) Tieing bundles
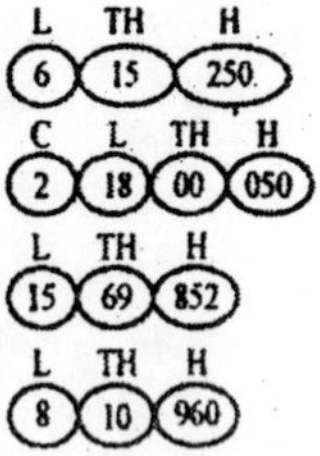
(c) Positioning
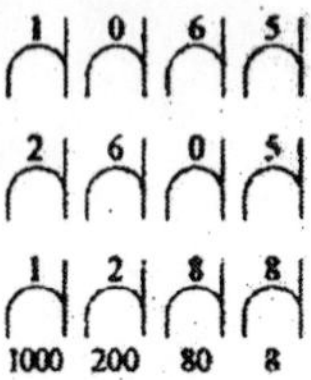
(d) Using different colours for different bundles
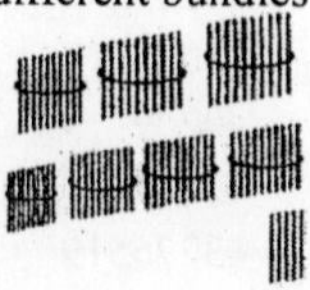</td></tr>
</table>

Problem	*Error*	*Reason*	*Strategy*
		Eg. : 8569	
Writing in numbers :			
Six hundred and fifteen	6015	Poor concept or place value	(i) Used tins or cans with numbers
Eight hundred and fifty one	8051	Lack of continuous drill	615 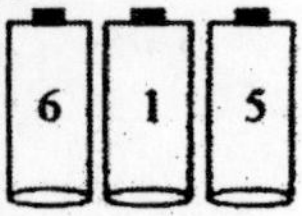
Two hundred and fifty two	20052, 2, 252 200052	Poor vocabulary	
		Poor reading ability	5209 
Four thousand two hundred and thirty	400530, 450030, 405030, 400050030	Confusion in place value	(ii) Inserters in boxes
Five thousand two hundred and nine	529, 502009 5000209		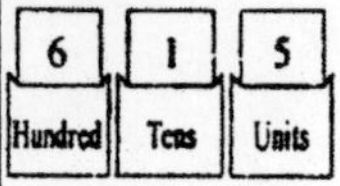 615 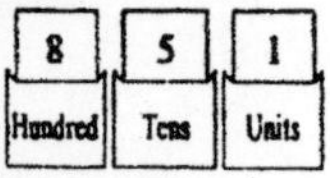 851
Ascending and descending order			
Write any 5 numbers that are (a) Lesser than 12 (b) Lesser than 18 arrange in increasing order	2, 3, 4, 5, 1 14, 16, 10, 8, 6 12, 13, 16, 14, 15 18, 19, 22, 24 18, 19, 20, 21, 22	- Difficulty in understanding the concept - Disorganisation - Short attention span - Inability to follow oral directions	Use of (1) Ascending and descending ladder 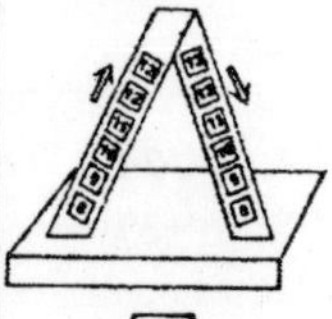
(a) 103, 390, 309, 121 (b) 6049, 2234, 6120, 2078	390, 309, 12, 103 309, 390, 103, 121 2078, 2079, 2089	- Failing to learn theory through examples - Confusion in terms of	

<table>
<tr><th>Problem</th><th>Error</th><th>Reason</th><th>Strategy</th></tr>
<tr><td></td><td>2078, 2234,
6049, 6120</td><td>increasing or
decreasing
numbers</td><td></td></tr>
<tr><td>Additions facts
4 + 2
4 + 4
5 + 2
5 + 5</td><td>4 + 2 = 5
4 + 4 = 0
5 + 2 = 4
5 + 5 = 11</td><td>- Lack of concept of symbols
- Unable to read the symbol
- Inability to learn things in a sequence
- Awkwardness in self expression
- Lack of number concept
- Poor retention of what has been studied
- Short attention span
- Lack of co-ordination
- On horizontal line addition facts are more difficult to comprehend</td><td>Use of straws/bamboo/Chalk/paperstrips/match sticks

|||| + ||
4+2=6
|||| + ||||
4+4=8
||||| + ||
5+2=7
||||| + |||||
5+5=10</td></tr>
<tr><td>Additions facts
5
6
3</td><td>5 | 5
+6 | +6
+3 | +3
11 | 11</td><td>Poor number concept

Lack of continous drill</td><td>5 |||||
+6 111111
+3 111
14 ||||||||||||||</td></tr>
<tr><td>24
+37</td><td>24 | 24
+37 | +37
60 | 34</td><td>Poor concept in the use of symbols and signs</td><td>24
+ 37
|| 61 ||||</td></tr>
<tr><td>56
+28</td><td>56
+28
86</td><td>Poor addition skills
Directionality problems solved from left to right</td><td>56
|||||+28 ||||||
|| 84 ||||||||</td></tr>
</table>

Problem	*Error*	*Reason*	*Strategy*
32 25 46 ———	32 | 32 25 | 25 46 | 46 —————— 96 | 911	||| 32 || || 25 ||||| |||| 46 |||||| ——— 103	
Add 15 + 27	15 + 27 = 35	Step I Tens | Ones 1 | 5 2 | 7 Think 5 + 7 = 12 12 = 1 ten + 2 ones	Step II Tens | Ones [1] | 1 | 5 2 | 7 Step III Tens | Ones 1 | 1 | 5 2 | 7 4 | 2
Add 17 + 18 =	17 + 18 = 25	First add the tens and ones separately Then if there are more than nine ones exchange ten ones for one ten. Before the exchange After the exchange	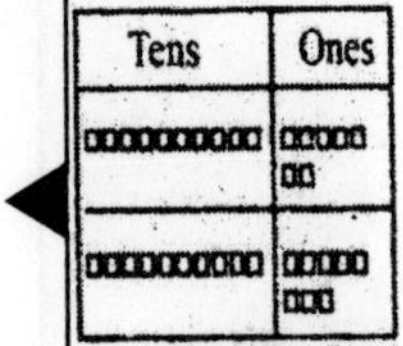 17 = 1 ten + 7 ones 18 = 1 ten + 8 ones 17+18 = 2 tens +15 ones 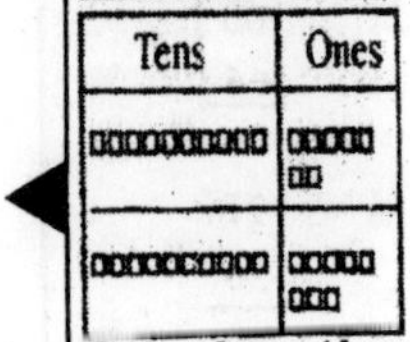 17+18 = 2 tens + 15 ones = 3 tens + 5 ones = 35

Problem	*Error*	*Reason*	*Strategy*
Subtraction			
4 - 3 5 - 3 7 - 5 8 - 4	4 - 3 = 3 5 - 3 = 8 7 - 5 = 3 8 - 4 = 5	Misconception Confusion Lack of attention Poor concept of symbols	Using bamboo/ straw/ice cream spoons  4 - 3 = 1 5 - 3 = 2 7 - 5 = 2 8 - 4 = 4 e.g. Using number line when we count backwards we substract
6 - 3 10 - 4 10 - 10	9 - 3 = 5 10 - 4 = 14 10 - 10 = 12	Problems with zero Difficulty in carrying over	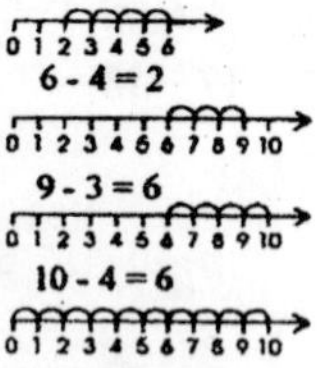 6 - 4 = 2 9 - 3 = 6 10 - 4 = 6 10 - 10 = 0
		Difficulty in getting proper change after monitory transactions	(a) Using seeds or buttons ●●●●● 51 ● -30 21
66 -66 77 -26	66 -66 126 77 -26 91	Adds for subtraction without taking into account the symbol involved	●●●●●● 66 ●●●●●● -66 00

Problem	*Error*	*Reason*	*Strategy*
Subtraction (continued) 86 -42	96 -42 123	No knowledge of regrouping Alternates columns. Problems with directionality	(b) Using colour differentiation 77 -26 64
108 -79	108 -79 31	Zero concept poor place value error	86 -42 44 108 -79 29
Subtract 43 -17	43 -17	43 -17 510	Another method 43=4 tens+3 ones 17=1 ten+7 ones To take away 17 we must take away 1 ten and 7 ones
		Before the exchange	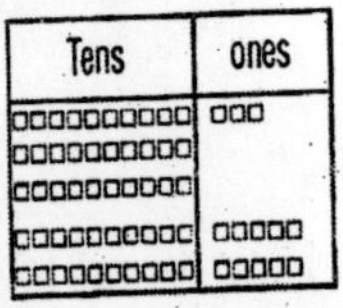 To have enough ones so that we can take away 7 ones exchange one ten for ten ones. Cross out a ten and draw 10 ones
		After the exchange	43=4 tens + 3 ones 17 = 1 ten + 7 ones 43-17=2 tens+6 ones = 26

Problem	*Error*	*Reason*	*Strategy*
Multiplication			
2 x 4	2 x 4 = 6	Cannot bring tables to memory and repeat sequentially	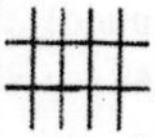 2 x 4 = 8
3 x 3	3 x 3 = 6		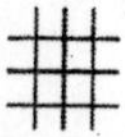 3 x 3 = 9
4 x 3	4 x 3 = 7		
		Rigidity of thought Poor concept Lack of drill	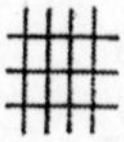 4 x 3 = 12
3 times Multiplication :		Poor memory Confusion due to lack of clarity	Using bamboo sticks/match sticks/ ice cream spoons
3 x 3	3 x 3 = 6		
3 x 7	3 x 7 = 20		
3 x 8	3 x 8 = 25		 3 x 1 3 x 1 3 x 1
			Step 1 : Some bamboo sticks are given to the students and made to tie bundles of 3 each
			Step 2 : Each bundle of 3 sticks is then counted as follows - Taking the first bundle of 3 3x=3 ie1+1+ +1=1 x 3 = 3 Taking two bundles it becomes 3 + 3 = 6 or 3 x 2 = 6 or 1+1+1=3 3 x 2 = 6 1+1+1 = 3 Similarly three bundles becomes

Problem	*Error*	*Reason*	*Strategy*
			3 x 3 = 9 for verification of the answer, the student can check as follows : 3x4=12 (3+3+3+3 = 12) as one takes four bundles of 3 sticks each.
Multiplication (continued)			
23 x3	23 x3 66	Cannot carry digits	
23 x4	23 x4 812	Incorrect processing Place value problem	2 x 3 = 6 tens 3 x 3 = 9 ones 2 x 3 tens = 60 3 x 3 ones = 9 69
32 x2	32 x2 54		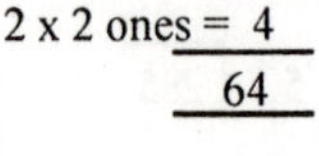 2 x 3 tens = 6 tens 2 x 2 ones = 4 ones 2 x 3 tens = 60 2 x 2 ones = 4 64
Division			
2 ⟌ 8	2 ⟌ 8 (quotient 8) 8 10	Carelessness Place value problem Sequencing problem Error in copying Poor concept Difficulty in memorising tables	2 ⟌ 8 (quotient 4) 8 0
3 ⟌ 9	3 ⟌ 9 (quotient 3) 6 3		3 ⟌ 9 (quotient 3) 9 0

Problem	*Error*	*Reason*	*Strategy*
4 ⟌12	1 4 ⟌21 4 4		3 4 ⟌12 12 0
Division (continued)			
4 ⟌86	41 4 ⟌86 41 24 24 0	Does not know to use reminders place value difficulty at the quotient level. Records the quotient first digit in the ones place. Does not record zero after dividing a number	21 4 ⟌86 8 6 4 2
7 ⟌473	19 7 ⟌473 7 73 73 0		67 7 ⟌473 42 53 49 4
8 ⟌72	7 8 ⟌72 56 4		9 8 ⟌72 72 0
Division (continued)			
5 ⟌285	417 5 ⟌285 20 8 5 35 35 0	Sequencing problem Missing steps while dividing Poor place value concept Confusion in substraction Basics poor	Divisor = Number used for dividing Dividend=number to be divided by the divisor Using bamboo Step 1 : The problem is first written down on paper Step 2 : Check if the first digit in

Problem	*Error*	*Reason*	*Strategy*
		Answer : 57 5)285 25 35 35 0	the dividend is greater than divisor 5 or less than that Step 3 : Since it is less than 5 the next digit is to be considered. The number then to be divided is 28. Step 4 : Each student is given 28 bamboo sticks, the divisor being 5, they are asked to make maximum bundles each containing 5 bamboo sticks. Each can then make only 5 bundles with 3, bamboos remaining thus 28 - 5 = 5 (5) + 3 5 5)285 25 35 Step 5 : The student then brings down the remaining digit (5) in the dividend writing it exactly next to the remainder (3) Step : Each student should then be given 35 bamboos thus again making maximum bundles of 5 each. Each student then makes exactily 7 bundles i.e. 7 x 5 = 35 5 (7) = 35

Concept of place value - simple clues :

Ten thousand	10,000	20,000	30,000	40,000	50,000
Thousands	1,000	2,000	3,000	4,000	5,000
Hundreds	100	200	300	400	500
Tens	10	20	30	40	50
Units	1	2	3	4	5

Place value concept in ascending and descending order used:

Ascending Order

Unit	*Tens*	*Hundreds*	*Thousands*	*Ten thousand*
0	0	0	0	0
1	10	100	1000	10000
2	20	200	2000	20000
3	30	300	3000	30000
4	40	400	4000	40000
5	50	500	5000	50000
6	60	600	6000	60000
7	70	700	7000	70000
8	80	800	8000	80000
9	90	900	9000	90000

Descending Order

Ten thousand	*Thousands*	*Hundreds*	*Tens*	*Unit*
10000	1000	100	10	1
20000	2000	200	20	2
30000	3000	300	30	3
40000	4000	400	40	4
50000	5000	500	50	5
60000	6000	600	60	6
70000	7000	700	70	7
80000	8000	800	80	8
90000	9000	900	90	9

Indian System

It will be easy to learn arithmetics if numbers are introduced to the children, as shown in the chart. Begin the counting from the right side i.e., from units (avoid sequential numbers after ten). Guide children to construct multi-digit numbers gradually. It is the easy, fast and better technique to introduce numbers to them.

Crores	*Ten Lakhs*	*Lakhs*	*Ten Thousands*	*Thousands*	*Hundreds*	*Tens*	*Unit*
10000000	1000000	100000	10000	1000	100	10	1
20000000	2000000	200000	20000	2000	200	20	2
30000000	3000000	300000	30000	3000	300	30	3
40000000	4000000	400000	40000	4000	400	40	4
50000000	5000000	500000	50000	5000	500	50	5
60000000	6000000	600000	60000	6000	600	60	6
70000000	7000000	700000	70000	7000	700	70	7
80000000	8000000	800000	80000	8000	800	80	8
90000000	9000000	900000	90000	9000	900	90	9

Western System

It will easy to learn arithmetic if we introduce numbers to the children, as shown in the chart. Begin the counting from the right side i.e., from units (Avoid sequential numbers after ten). Guide children to construct multi-digit numbers grandually. It is the easy, fast and better technique to introduce numbers to them.

Millions thousands	*Hundred thousands*	*Ten*	*Thousands*	*Hundreds*	*Tens*	*Unit*
9000000	900000	90000	9000	900	90	9
8000000	800000	80000	8000	800	80	8
7000000	700000	70000	7000	700	70	7
6000000	600000	60000	6000	600	60	6
5000000	500000	50000	5000	500	50	5
4000000	400000	40000	4000	400	40	4
3000000	300000	30000	3000	300	30	3
2000000	200000	20000	2000	200	20	2
1000000	100000	10000	1000	100	10	1
0	0	0	0	0	0	0

Mathematical "PROBES"

ADDITION

Count and write the numbers

Eg.

a 3 

b 

c 

1)

a 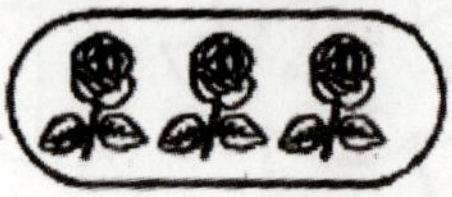

b 

c 

2)

a 

b 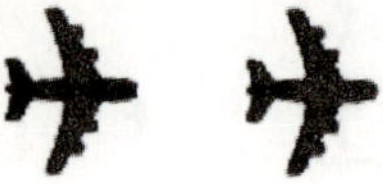

c 

3)

Shade the items as indicated by the number on the right

Eg. 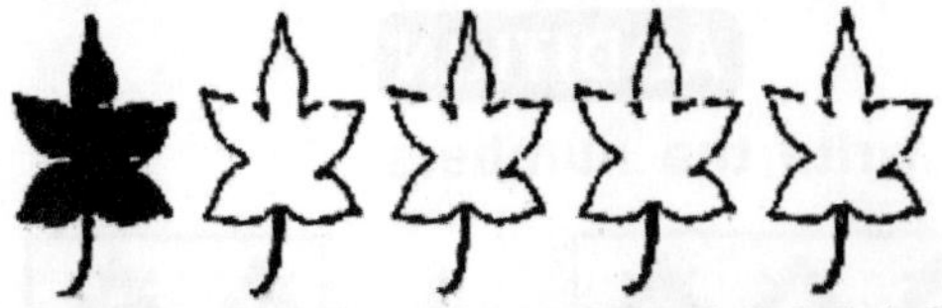 1

a  4

b  5

This is how you can add numbers. Complete the following

Eg. 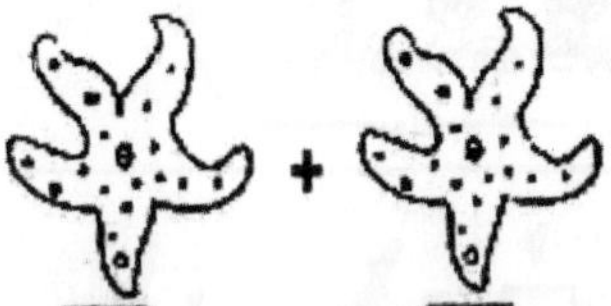

1 + 1 = 2

a 

2 + ☐ = ☐

b 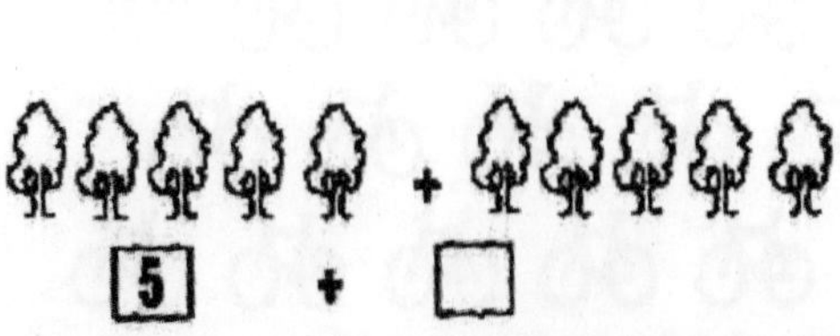

5 + ☐ = ☐

Add the number of items in each of the following sets

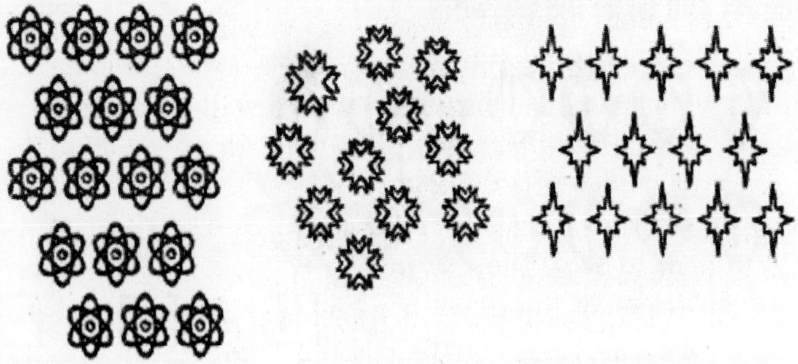

a ☐ b ☐ c ☐

d ☐

Classroom observation

Count the number of

a) Students in your class ☐

b) Windows in the classroom ☐

c) Tables in the classroom ☐

d) Pictures on the wall ☐

Subtraction

Subtract and write the answers

a

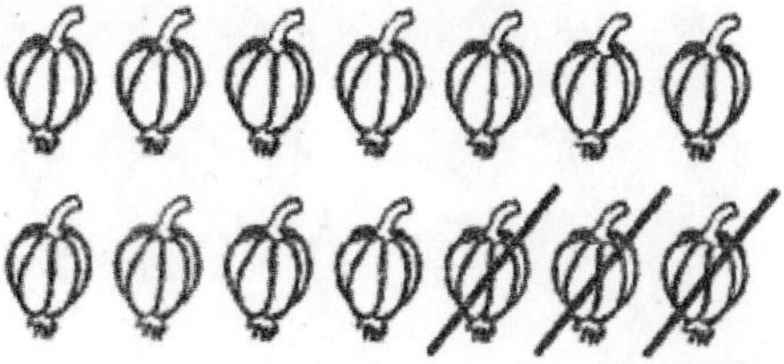

14 — 3 = ☐

b

32 — 12 = ☐

c

12 — 4 = ☐

d

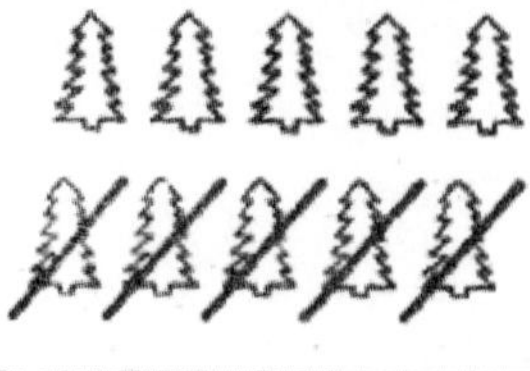

10 — 5 = ☐

e

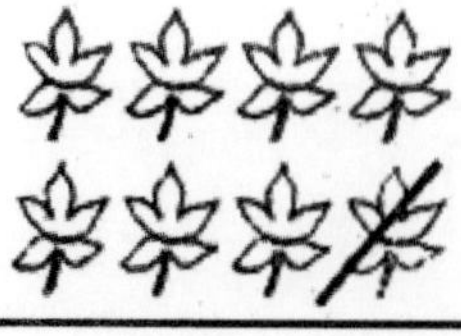

8 — 1 = ☐

How much do you remember

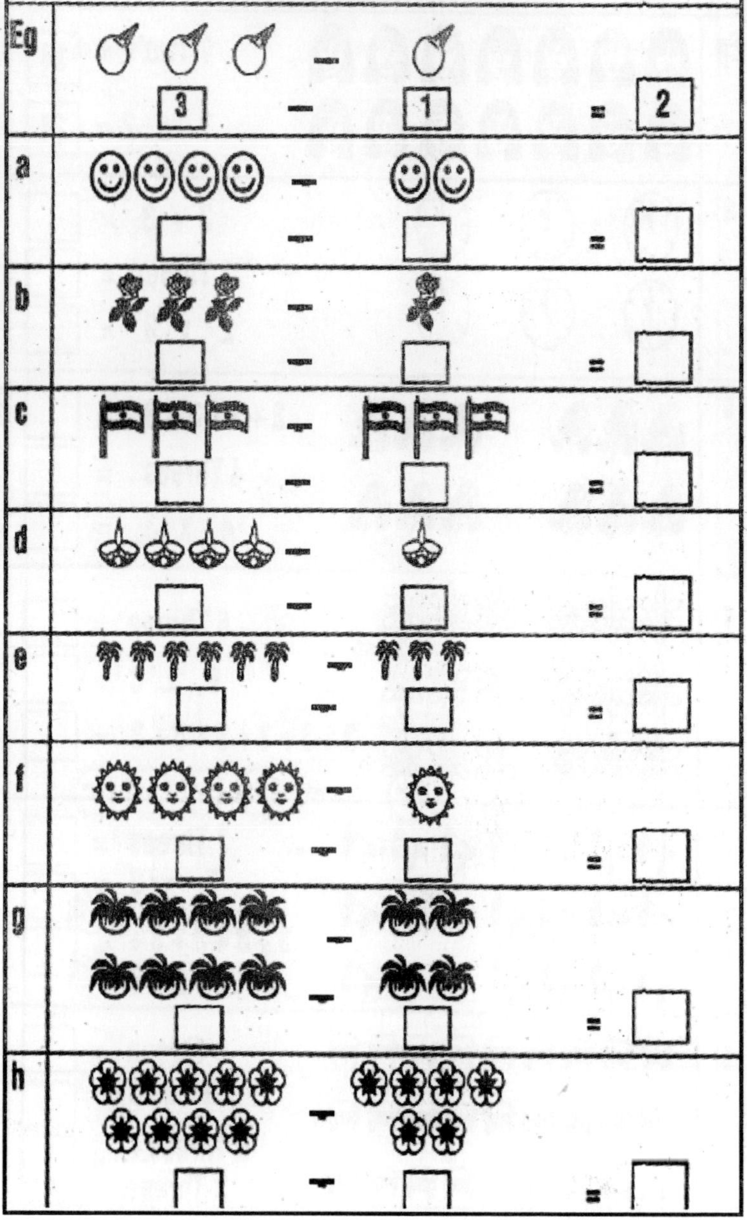

Multiplication

Multiply and write the answers

Eg		7 Two's = 14 7 x 2 = 14
a		3 + 3 = ☐ 2 Threes = ☐ 2 x 3 = ☐
b		3+3+3+3 = ☐ 4 Threes = ☐ 4 x 3 = ☐
c		6 Threes = ☐ 6 x 3 = ☐ 3+3+3+3+3+3 = ☐
d	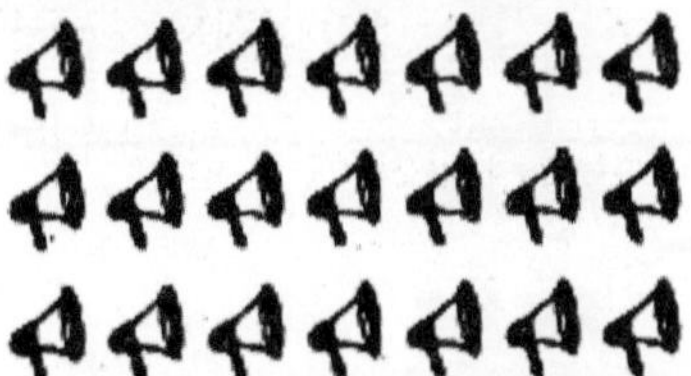	7 Threes = ☐ 7 x 3 = ☐ 3+3+3+3+ 3+3+3 = ☐
e		9 Threes = ☐ 9 x 3 = ☐ 6 Threes + 3 Threes = ☐

Colour the following

a) 5 apples

b) 2 bananas

c) 6 pumpkins

d) 3 Carrots

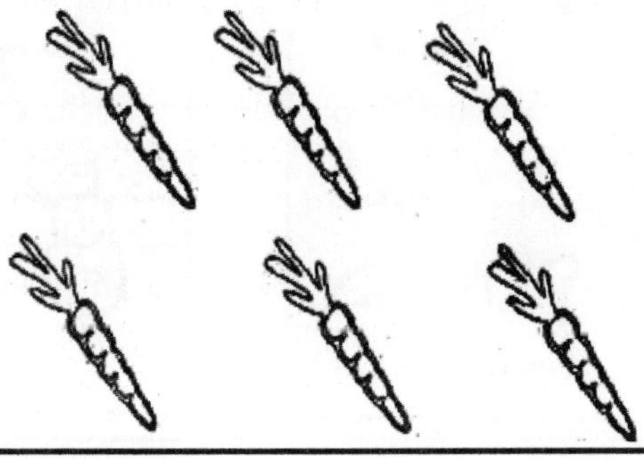

Match the pairs of equivalent sets with lines

Division

Fill the missing number in the box

$2 \div \square = 2$

$6 \div \square = 3$

$10 \div 2 = \square$

$14 \div 7 = \square$

$8 \div \square = 4$

$16 \div 8 = \square$

Good $\square$

Fair $\square$

Poor $\square$

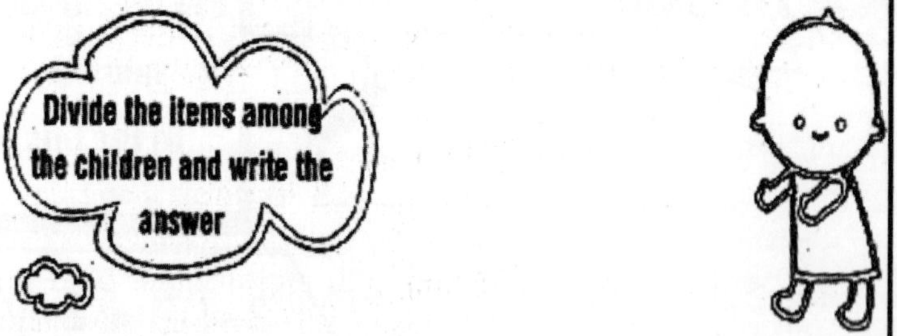

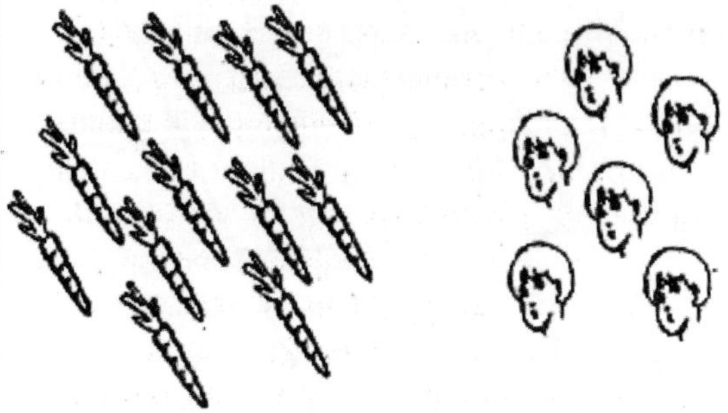

12 ÷ 6 = ☐

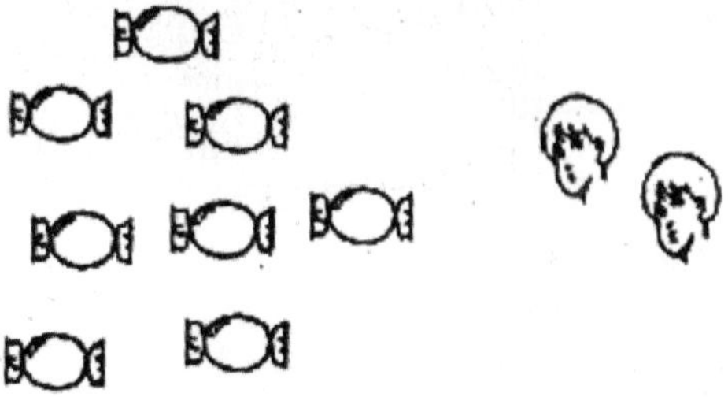

8 ÷ 2 = ☐

Tick ( ) the correct answer

16 ÷ 8

2 8 9

49 ÷ 7

6 7 9

48 ÷ 8

4 6 8

18 ÷ 3

2 4 6

40 ÷ 10

2 4 5

30 ÷ 5

5 4 6

Distribute the mangoes equally among the monkeys

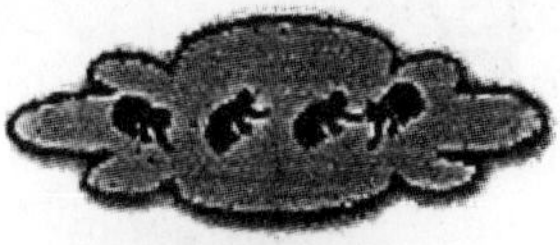

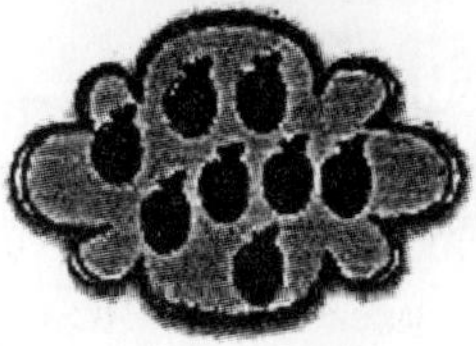

One monkey will get _________ mangoes

Divide and draw a line to the correct answer

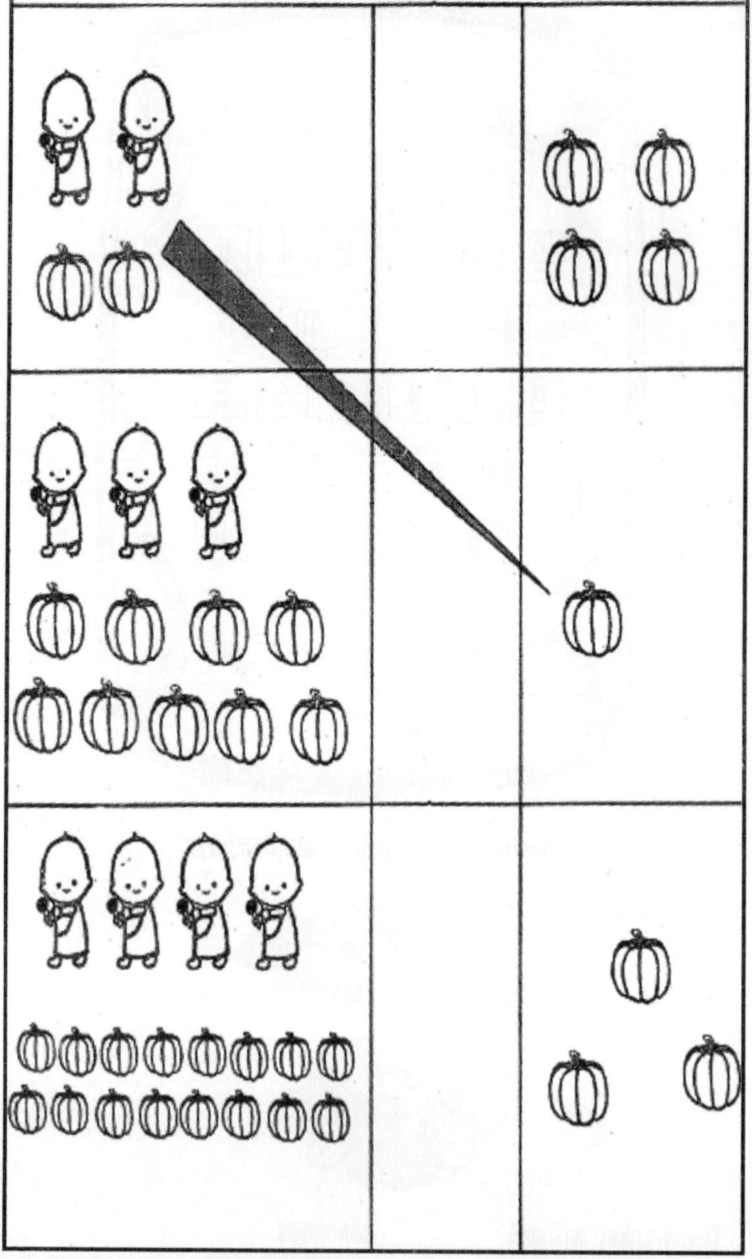

Fill the missing numbers by multiplying

a. 8 x 2 = 16

b. .... x 3 = 12

c. .... x 4 = 20

d. 4 x .... = 28

e. 3 x 3 = ...

f. 6 x .... = 30

a. 3 x 2 x 4 = 24

b. 4 x .... x 5 = 40

c. .... x 5 x 10 = 100

d. 6 x 2 x .... = 108

e. 0 x 8 x 2 = ...

Fill the missing numbers by multiplying

2 □	2 □	5 □	6 □	□ 3
x 2	x 5	x 7	x 8	x 9
4 2	105	357	496	117

Study each picture, write multiplication and division answer for each	
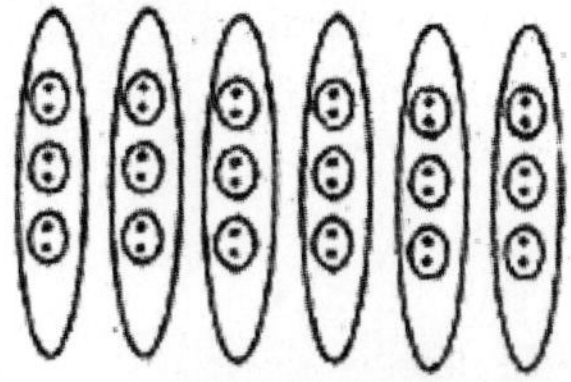	6 x 3 = 18 18 ÷ 3 = 6
	4 x 4 = □ 16 ÷ 4 = □
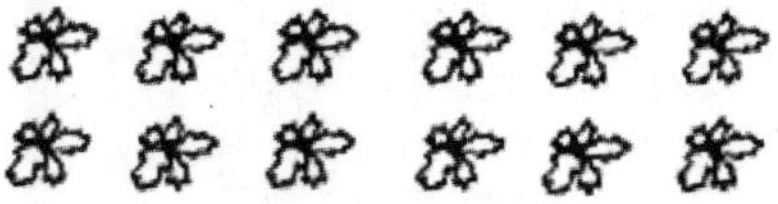	12 x 2 = □ 12 ÷ 2 = □
	5 x 5 = □ 25 ÷ = □
	3 x 3 = □ ÷ 3 = □
	8 x 2 = □ 16 ÷ 4 = □

Teaching basic concepts in mathematics through kolam patterns (A traditional design used in floor decoration)

Ascending and descending order

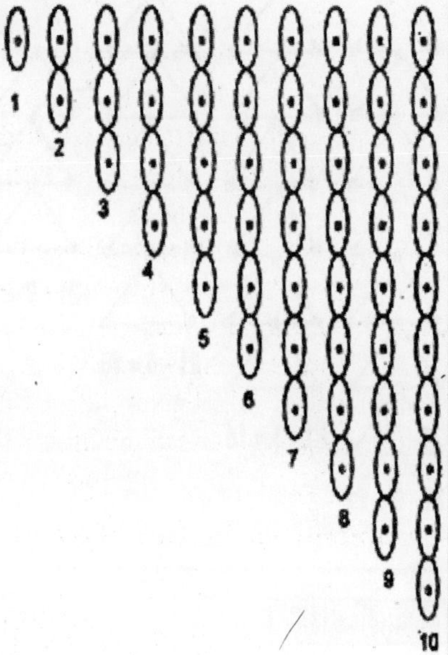

Addition

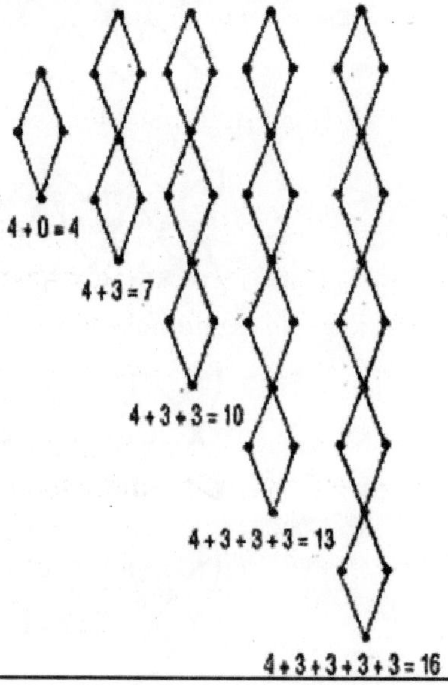

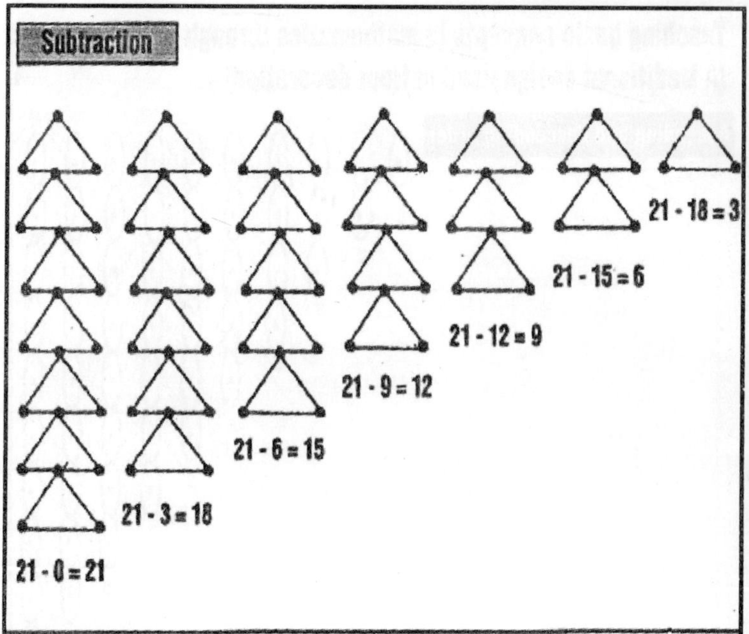
Subtraction
21 - 18 = 3
21 - 15 = 6
21 - 12 = 9
21 - 9 = 12
21 - 6 = 15
21 - 3 = 18
21 - 0 = 21

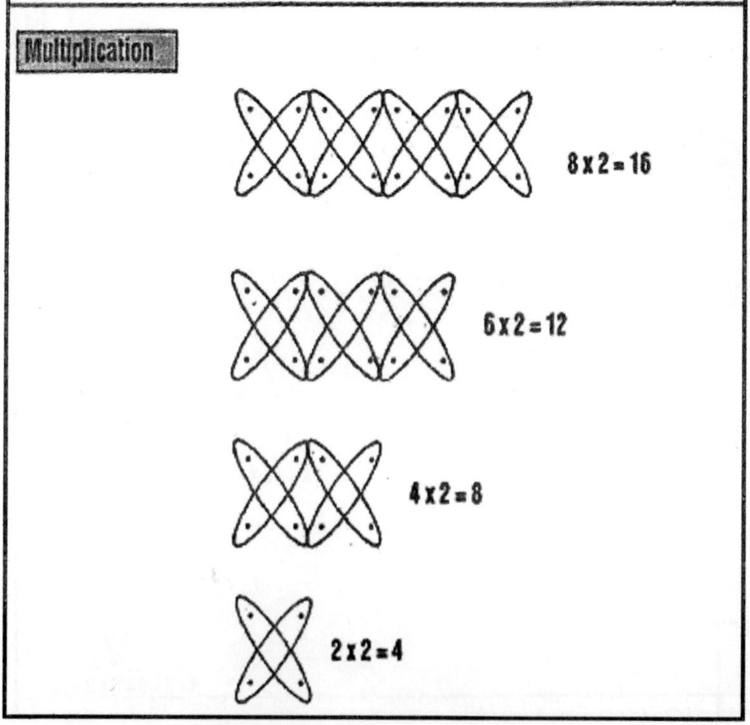
Multiplication
8 x 2 = 16
6 x 2 = 12
4 x 2 = 8
2 x 2 = 4

6

Guidelines for Teachers and Parents

Children need guidance and sympathy far more than instruction

- Anne Sullivan

Preparing children to school is the sole responsibility of parents since they must he ready to learn from the first day of school.

Most children do well in school, they may be able to learn quickly, recall facts and gradually keep pace of the essentials that need to be understood and learnt. Some children do not do so well. They may have difficulty in paying attention resulting in poor academic achievement.

WHY THE DIFFERENCE IN PERFORMANCE AMONG CHILDREN?

Research has revealed that it is the behavior and attitude that interferes with learning rather than IQ. Children who are successful at academics have the right attitude, are motivated, pay attention, are relaxed and can ignore distractions that may interfere with learning. None of these are inborn but can be learnt and acquired with guidance from teachers and parents.

Some of the skills that need to be developed in children in helping them to prepare for their daily classroom tasks and as well as to give the needed confidence in preparing for the exams include;

> Developing good study habits

It is very important to develop and follow a particular time schedule for study. Children may need guidance in terms what and how to start. Therefore it is always satisfying to start with, something that is easier for them to learn and that which is interesting. Remember to have a specific area set aside with least distractions but at the same time provide comfort.

> **Motivate to concentrate**

This can be achieved by bringing in a little change in the activity. Provide variety with sensory stimulation, Introduce small games to keep the tempo of learning.

Relate the learning material to the child's needs. Parents can set the goal for learning at the same time enable the child to develop his own plan of action. Discuss each goal. Remember that many small goals, one after another are better than a single large goal.

> **Create curiosity**

This is perhaps the greatest of all motivations. Let the main theme or idea be presented with solutions be taught and later let the child practice and seek answers to the problem. This will naturally arouse the curiosity in the child to succeed.

> **Develop questioning skills**

With the process of questioning starts the thinking process.When child begin to ask themselves questions like how? what? why? their alertness and interest in the working situation increases.Thus encourage them to the task of self questioning. This helps children to focus their attention while studying. Asking questions can bring back wandering attention.

> **Create a desire to learn**

Start initiating into the lesson by working along with the child, talking about what is being learnt and how it would be useful. Spend time with the child in making him comprehending its benefits or usefulness.

Put up meaningful posters to re-emphasize facts.

> **Keeping them interested**

Learning is a joint effort. Everyone must help children to learn. Teachers are responsible for teaching and parents for parenting, but students must realize that no one else can do their learning for them.

Children must believe that the hours spent studying and the effort they put into it make the difference between success and failure.

You can help children accept the fact that their efforts do make a difference. The next time they bring home test results, written comments, or report cards discuss the reasons why they did well or poorly. Help them relate their efforts to the result.

> Inculcate a sense of responsibility

Make the child understand his responsibility for learning. At the same time it is the parent/teachers responsibility to create the best possible climate for learning to take place:An effective method would be to involve the child- by questioning.

What they expect to learn?
What would be the outcome on completion?
What would they do to achieve the results?

> Use praise and recognition

Do reward the child for improvement. Your praise is like music to his ears. You might consider treats or trips or privileges for their earnest achievements. This would foster in the child a feeling of self confidence and indicates an acknowledgment for his efforts and capabilities.

In a regular classroom situation this serves a form of recognition and encouragement to the child and further contributes to their own learning.

> Using self talk and positive images

In order to pay attention to the task children can learn the knack of doing it. Never threaten or order them.

Children can use words or phrases to help control attention. For example, they can tell themselves to keep their eyes on the black board while the teacher is writing on it to explain problems. You can help them practice positive self talk at home in various situations when playing a game, helping around the house, or working at a hobby.

Help them stop negative self talk (it's hopeless) and to be positive about themselves to say, "I can do it". Positive self talk might include the slogan "**Quitters don't win and winners don't quit**".

> Encourage at every small step

One of the most effective technique is to let the child know that you have the trust and belief that he would accomplish the task assigned. A word of encouragement on a failure is worth more than a whole lot of praise after a success.

Make the child to understand that no one is perfect and by learning something for a short while we may not be perfect at it. Best results are achieved with repeated attempts and success.

> Use cooperative learning situations

Competition introduced into the teaching learning environment improves performance but not always learning. Competitive situations can be fun for short intervals of time. Group students to have a mix of high and low achievers is important. This method can be used for any subject matter learning in the regular class room.

> Employ multi - sensory approach

A varied use of techniques creates an interesting learning environment chart, pictures, picture books, cartoons, films, video films puzzles, CD, power point presentation and over head transparency may be used to introduce colour and variety to the content being taught.

A myriad of audio techniques can be used such as playing music, creating ones own rhythm and music occasionally recorded cassettes material may be given.

Kinesthetic techniques involves providing real hands on experience to the child. Sand trays may be used for learning alphabets, numerals, spellings etc. Cutting and pasting pictures, drawing and painting, doing small projects are some of the innumerable exercises that can be used to provide kinesthetic experiences.

Remembering

Research has shown that a child's success in school is determined not just by intelligence but by strategies he or she uses to master many facts and ideas.

Understanding a subject doesn't happen. It takes work. It requires taking an interest in the subject and relating new information to familiar information.

Besides teaching the various strategies for paying attention, you can help your child use various strategies to remember.You can decide how best to adapt to a particular strategy by making inferences.

TIPS FOR HELPING CHILDREN PREPARE FOR TESTS

Taking a test can be very stressful for any child. Helping them prepare may help to reduce some of their anxiety and frustration especially when they feel they have spent plenty of time preparing for the same. However, it is not the number of hours that is put in — it is the quality of studying that is accomplished during those hours. Some strategies and tips to help children cope with test anxiety include

- **Make note cards**

When writing note cards the child is actively reviewing the information. Preparing these cards at home allows them to participate in extra curricular activities and to prepare anywhere without carrying heavy notes and textbooks.

Encourage them to write the questions or phrases on one side and corresponding answers on the other for the visual learners use coloured pens to relate ideas and themes.

- **Write practice test**

Anxious moments experience during a test is because of the limitation of time. Practice test enables them to face the pressure with ease. Prepare previous question papers can be tried out or a quiz allows them to gain familiarity with the format, terms or words.

The important aspect in writing such tests is to time the students for completion making him aware of the time required for the same. Encourage them to have enough time at the end to check through the answers.

- **Play games**

For children who find it monotonous to sit still at a table and read notes often do not use their time effectively due to various distractions. For such children learning through games may help to kindle their interest.

- **Incorporating technology and multimedia**

Technology is becoming an increasingly relevant part of student's lives. Find out best ways to utilize technologies and multimedia in the regular classroom or at home. Commercially available CD's for various subjects available may be effectively used to make learning interesting.

HOW CAN I HELP MY CHILD AT HOME

> Make directions specific and simple

Be sure you have your child's attention be brief and precise, give one direction at a time, later you may increase the complexity of the directions.

> Help your child get organized

Have a place for everything, establish routines and stick to them, when it needs to be altered the time to explain the change and "walk your child through", the new procedure. Provide work charts and check lists as reminders.

> Repeat learning experiences

Spellings and multiplication tables may be difficult, therefore repeat these tasks and try out other approaches such as multi sensory, writing words or tables on paper on sand or you may record it in a tape recorder and playback as and when required.

> Help your child learn how to learn

Making learning fun and enjoyable through games and varied experiences. Try different modes as telling, sharing doing the task in different ways, making up songs or rhymes create a study center for your child and teach study skills (read, recite, review, answer, questions, review again) Use hands on experiences to teach number and word skills.

> Communicate frequently with school

Allow time to share experiences with teacher and carry through the same approaches at home, find out means of assistances that could be availed form teachers and peers.

> Keep expectations and goals attainable

Start with small goals that your child is capable of achieving and once accomplished increase the expectation level, choose expectation that emphasize your child's strength, place your child in "**win**" situations as often as possible to enhance his self esteem.

> Establish clear rules and consequences

Write rules as well as consequences for breaking the rules (i.e. home work must be completed, checked and corrected before watching TV). Discuss rules with your child and paste them at conspicuous place, follow through consistently with consequences, avoid nagging reminding, negotiating or making expectations.

> Acknowledge the child's frustrations

Let your child know you understand his difficulties and say something like "I know it is hard for you, you are trying hard, you can do it better"

> Praise and encourage the activities which your child excels

A word of praise and encouragement can really boost the child's sense of self esteem and accomplishments, they may be sensitive to criticism easily discouraged and over dependent —but they can be taught to compensate to have self confidence and to be independent.

> Model and role play social situations with your child

Prepare your child for situations, he is likely to encounter, by talking about it and ways to handle it, at the same time you may role play the situations and solutions for the same.

> Reward your child for appropriate behaviour

Acknowledge achievements use encouragement, praise, hug and rewards, these children often endure so much criticism, impatience, frustrations and shame that they need positive feed back and reinforcement as much as possible.

References

* Crealock, E. and Kronick, D. (1993). *Children and Young People with Specific Learning Disabilities.* Guide for Special Education, 9, Paris, UNESCO, 1-57.
* Mercer, C. D. (1983). *Students with Learning Disabilities,* (2nd, ed.), London, Charles, E. Merill Publishing House, 340-350.
* Mercer, C. D. and Miller, S.P. (1992). *Teaching students with learning problems in math to acquire, understand and apply basic math facts. Remedial and Special Educate,* 13(3): 19-35.
* Sarojini Devi, P. (1997. July 1). *Teacher Training Warrants Scrutiny.* The Hindu, 26.
* Starr, J. W. (1969). *The Teaching of Mathematics in the Elementary School,* Pennsylva. International Text Book Company.
www.wpic.ovg.

7

Review of Literature

The literature pertaining to the present investigation has been reviewed under the following heads :

(A) Learning Disability Among Primary School Children - Emerging Concepts and Trends

(B) Learning Disability With Special Reference to Dyscalculia

(C) Arithmetic Competence Deficits and its Impact on Children

(D) Remediation of Dyscalculic Children - Means and Methods

(E) Teachers' Role in Remediation

(A) Learning Disability Among Primary School Children - Emerging Concepts and Trends

School experience constitutes a major social influence on behaviour (Berk, 1994 and Ghose, 1996). For children, schooling occupies a high proportion of working hours during much of their growing years. As a result, this system is called upon to provide a variety of experiences to meet the growth needs and to enhance growth partnership between home and the school (Gokaran, 1989; Ujjwalarani and Kumari, 1994 and Rao and Parthasarathy, 1995).

The Department of Social Welfare and UNICEF (1994) report that over 3.5 million children of school age (6 - 14 years) are out of school. They are neither enrolled nor dropped out. About 19 per cent children enrolled in class I drop out before they complete five years of primary school, while 40 percent drop out before class VIII (Child Asia, 1993).

A child quits school not on account of one reason, but because of a constellation of reasons (Pangotra, 1986; Singh, 1986; Clairns et al., 1989 and Barrett and Trevitt, 1991). Poor achievement and lack of interest are the major reasons for dropping out. Studies have shown that more than half the children in class IV and class V fail to meet basic requirements of literacy and numeracy (Patyal, 1980 and Newman, 1989 and Bhagat, 1993).

Projecting the rural scenario of primary education as it prevails, Acharya (1988), Newman (1989) and Sohoni (1990) indicate that the National Education Policy (1986) did not refer to the vast bulk of rural primary schools, where 77 first graders out of 100 enrolled, drop out before they reach class VIII where 40 per cent of the buildings are of temporary quality; 40 per cent of schools have no blackboards; 59 per cent have no drinking water and 35 per cent function with only a single teacher.

Krishnamurthy (1993) and Rani and Bhadramani (1993) report that of the 100 million children attending primary classes, 50 per cent of them achieve only 30 per cent scores. On the other hand, some children with normal IQ and adequate adaptive function nevertheless have difficulty in learning to read, write or do arithmetics (Hayes, 1995).

Analyzing the infrastructure of the primary schools and the poor quality performance of the children, Brenam (1982) and Rush and Vitale (1994) recommend that the first task of development in schools must be to ensure that children with special education needs are discovered as early as possible. The most vital intervention should begin between the ages of 7 and 8 years and for this the teachers should become aware of early signs of emerging difficulties and be skilled in resolving them at a stage where the children are amenable to ordinary classroom approaches (Lernor et al., 1981; Peer, 1996).

Adelman (1992), Rush and Vitale (1994) emphasize the need to identify factors that lead students to become at risk for school failure. Absenteeism, academic failure and early school departure are links in a long chain of interconnected problems. The NIPCCD (1994) concurs that dropping out is a progression of factors that begin at primary level up to the student's final decision.

Elia et al. (1993) refer to American Psychiatric Association (1987) that lists academic under achievement as characteristic of most children with attention deficit hyperactivity disorder (ADHD) and school failure. Matsuura et al. (1993) investigated emotional and behavioural problems among primary school children using Rutters questionnaire in Japan (N = 2638), China (N = 2432) and Korea (N = 1975). The results indicated higher prevalence of deviance among boys and among those children with poor school achievement.

Pandey and Advani (1995) and Weldon (1996) observed that even mildly dyslexic children or those with specific learning difficulties tend to have low self-esteem and its effect spreads through the social and academic world. Among the other associated conditions, Lefrancois (1983), Epstein and Cullinan (1984), Bruck (1987) and Stevenson et al. (1993), explain that if learning problems lead to behaviour problems, hyperactivity is likely to emerge.

Classroom behaviour is the outcome of a complex set of factors operating on students at different levels (Esser et al., 1990; Menon, 1995 and Bayrd, 1996). Inadequate housing facilities and abnormal family size, disturbed family situation may hinder pupils' performance. Over population and environmental pollution may increase behavioural disorders among individuals. In addition, performance in the examination emphasized as success parameter, is one of the major reasons for undesirable behaviour pattern among students.

One of the major obstacles in creating an effective classroom environment is the behavioral problem child, who cannot adjust to the socially acceptable norms of behaviour and consequently disrupts his own academic progress, the learning efforts of his classmate and inter-personal relations (George and Sananda Raj, 1983; Sinha, 1988; McIntosh et al., 1993 and Menon, 1995).

In a study on socio-metric status and behaviour of 179 children aged 8-12 years, including 36 children with learning disability, Nabuzoka and Smith (1993) nominated the Learning Disabled (L.D.) children as shy, rejected, seeking help and as victims of bullying significantly more than non-learning disabled children. Greshna (1982), Dudley - Marling (1985), Larry (1989) and Sharma (1993) also have similar view on the poor social status of the learning disabled.

Prasad's (1982) study with primary school children showed that poor expressive language development and poor visual perceptual development as primary factors that led to learning difficulties. Sinha (1988) further adds that children enter school with behaviour problems that are not conducive to optimum learning.

Efforts continue to explore the cause of learning disabilities. Disturbances in the brains' information processing system occur prenatally, during birth or in the early years. An expectant mother's poor diet or use of drugs, alcohol, or cigarettes may restrict the blood supply and reduce oxygen to the foetal brain. Loss of oxygen can also result from a difficult delivery (Shields, 1989). Researches have found a link between specific learning problems and low birth weight, resulting from insufficient prenatal development of portions of the brain or foetal hypoximia (The Child's Rights Bulletin, 1996).

Cognizing the fact that the world disabled population would be well over 600 million by the end of this century (40% being school age children), Mckay (1994), Sethia et al. (1994) and Hayes (1995) highlight early recognition and intervention to help children with learning difficulty to overcome feelings of lowered self-esteem, self-hood and stress and to feel valued and integrated with the school system and the family (Rutter, 1985).

Milton (1993) contends that corporal punishment had only a negative effect on children's attitude to schooling though meant to induce academic progress among children (Rani and Bhadramani, 1993; Rao and Parthasarathy, 1996).

Wolff (1989) and Venugopal (1994) report studies relating to home environment and intellectual competence. They have shown that parents'educational level and the mothers tested intelligence are strongly related to the children's tested abilities from the age of 18 months onwards. However, the variety of stimulating experiences made an independent contribution (Desai, 1989; India, 1990; Kajjari and Khadi, 1994; and Mackey, 1996).

UNICEF (1988), Grolnick and Slowiaczek (1994); Pandey and Advani (1995) and the World Bank (1995) reiterate that the family is the most important channel of assistance to the child. However, today parents face the problem of rearing their children to face an extremely competitive world with knowledge. Anantharaman and Parthasarathy (1992), Desai (1994) and Pillowalla (1993) exhort that quite a few parents are involved and concerned about their children and play a positive role.

Balachandran (1993) states that parents willingly carry half the burden of educating the child and the problems with most underachievers are directly linked to lack of concentration. Cognizing the dependence of young children on the immediate environment, Subramanyam (1993), Gokaran (1989), Grotberg (1995) and the Mackey (1996) emphasize the role of the home, the neighborhood and the school to meet their growth needs and to provide the transfer of cultural values information and skills.

Research concerning the learning disabled. Students' spontaneous use of language in natural and contrived settings by Bryan et al. (1981), Dudley-Marling (1985) and Scarborough (1990) demonstrate that children with learning disabilities differ from their peers in "what they say and how they say if". They have shorter utterances (Donahue et al., 1982), provide less information (Knight-Arest, 1984) and request information less often when compared to normally achieving children.

Problems related to directionality, mirror writing, poor auditory discrimination, number order, clumsiness and difficulty in understanding instructions are some of the activities depicting specific disabilities (Ramaa, 1992; Ahuja, 1996). Bamman (1989), Farr (1989) and Bishop and Adams (1990) predict that a child who has specific reading language impairment in the preschool is at risk for specific reading disability in the later years.

Cognitive processing deficits are associated with learning disability. Sethia et al. (1994) list them as impairments related to short-term memory, long term memory, sequential memory, working memory, recall and recognition as quite common.

A comparative study with normally achieving students by Parmer et al. (1994) indicate that both students with mental retardation and those with learning disabilities lag considerably behind their average achieving peers. To Rao (1998) three mandatory characteristics by which L.D. can be identified include 'average' or 'above average intelligence', 'adequate sensóry acuity' and 'achievement considerably less than their composite IQ', 'age' and 'educational opportunity'.

Another area of motor behaviour which may signal a learning problem is co-ordination problem, synchronizing large muscles, fine motor tasks in writing, printing, drawing, copying and tracing (Lovitt, 1989) and handedness (Arnold and Askew, 1993).

Reports of Wong (1985) and Pressley et al. (1989) reveal that children with learning disabled frequently lack specific or general problem solving ability, they do not process information or apply knowledge effectively, experience difficulty in selecting and deploying task appropriate strategies and lack self-regulation processes.

Khurana (1988), Sharma (1993) and Ramaa (1997) list the characteristics of these children as one who pays attention to everything that goes on around him, cannot assign priorities to tasks for completion and is indiscriminate - a characteristic of immaturity. Response and behaviour of these children though not abnormal, are often more appropriate to much younger children. They also lack many of the basic skills usually acquired in preschool years, the foundations necessary to academic learning. Hyperactive behaviour may be exhibited in instructional settings by a short attention span, restlessness and exaggerated behaviour (Stevenson et al., 1993).

Mohan and Gulati (1986) and Sumangala (1995) observed correlation between academic achievement and intelligence. Both environmental and psychological factors play a significant role in the child's academic achievement. It is also felt that what is true about preventing disability equally holds good in promoting development. One needs to act early enough since the foundation of growth and development through the years of school age, youth and adult life is laid in early childhood have not been ruled out (Ganapathy and Singh, 1981 and Diamond et al., 1994).

If early years suffer relative neglect as they often do, it will not be early to make up later for the lost human potential (Kaul, 1986). Sinha (1991) and Narayan (1994) contend that by making primary education child oriented, the system might turn to be a joyful, inventive and satisfying learning activity rather than a system of rote and cheerless authoritarian instruction.

(B) Learning Disability with Special Reference to Dyscalculia

Learning disability is a fast expanding field, though much of it remain unexplored. They debate on learning disability till date relates to differing opinions as to what is really meant by the term 'learning disability' in terms of degree, nature of disability and identification procedures among other factors.

Following paragraphs reflect learning disabilities as explained in the educational sphere:

Learning disabilities irrespective of either physical, mental or learning conditions are universal across all ages, socio-economic levels and races with the individual facing mild or severe learning problem (Ramanujam, 1995).

Various definitions on learning disability are in vogue. According to Heward and Orlansky (1998), Shields (1989) and Rourke and Del Detto (1994) the term 'learning disability' refers to children with significant learning problems that cannot be explained by mental retardation, sensory impairment, emotional disturbance or lack of opportunity to learn.

According to Sarangi (1989) any average or above average child having academic performance below the norm is labeled as learning disabled. Ramaa (1992) refers to learning disability as the child's limited ability in learning.

Thomas et al. (1987) and Adams (1990) observe that students with learning disabilities display substantially greater number of error responses in certain academic subjects than their non-handicapped peers. While sources of backwardness are many, Menon and Koshy (1991) perceive two broad distinctions between one group of children - slow learners (IQ < 45 to 50) who by nature have limited intellectual endowment and the other group 'underachievers' (IQ - 75 and above), whose achievements are expressed by causes other than low mental ability.

Alexander (1993) and Bhatia (1996) remark that there are a substantial number of children delayed or retarded in learning to talk, in language acquisition or have great difficulty in learning to read, spell, write or calculate arithmetic problems. However, not all children with these problems have a learning disability per se.

Hallahan (1992) and Palmar et al. (1994) indicate that students with mental retardation and those with learning disabilities fall considerably behind their average peers, the latter having IQ scores from slightly below average to average with discrepancies in performance between two or more academic areas.

Harris and Liebert (1987) and Rao (1988) are of the view that the term learning disability is used when a child's school achievement is well below expectations, given the child's IQ score, family background and physical and emotional health are good.

Narayan (1994) noticed that dyslexia or dyscalculic, conditions that are purely academic oriented do not get detected in many individuals and they struggle a lot. This is because no survey on learning disabled children has been done due to probably the inconspicuous and misunderstood nature of the disability.

According to Witt et al. (1988), dyscalculia is a term that was originally used in medicine to indicate the virtual loss of mathematical ability after head trauma and was borrowed by some educators to describe basic arithmetic learning disorders. As contended by Podder, (1996) the loss of arithmetic ability to learn number and number relationships is 'dyscalculia'.

Differentiating the terms 'arithmetics' and 'mathematics' Lewis et al. (1989) states that 'arithmetics' is primarily concerned with computation - addition, subtraction, multiplication, division and algorithms related to these operations. 'Mathematics' includes computation, problem solving, estimation, approximation, prediction, application of concepts as in reading graphs, charts and tables.

Mercer (1983) considers arithmetics a universal language enabling people to think, record and communicate the elements and relationships involving quantity. It includes both verbal and written symbols that denote size, order relationship, space, form, distance and time (Geatheart and Gearheart, 1989; Mercer and Miller, 1992). Daily living requires the application of mathematic skills, for example, planning and monitoring time, computing percentages, making estimations, measuring textile purchase, computing scores, playing games etc. In school settings, problems in mathematics often result in school failure leading to high levels of anxiety. Further, successful functioning in the adult world requires a variety of problem solving skills that demands skills more than computation (Koscinski and Gast, 1993; Kulak, 1993).

Gakhar (1983) and Berk (1994) are of the view that mathematical reasoning like reading builds on a foundation of informally acquired knowledge. Research conducted by Woodward and Haward (1994) indicate that one of distinguishable feature of low achievers is their incapacity to use a range of representation systems (e.g. - drawing) when confronted with novel problems.

Batchelor et al. (1990) investigated neuropsychological factors as predictors of 1,1189 L.D. students' (aged 9-16 years) performance on visual and verbal arithmetic performance. Results suggest that students' arithmetic performance varied as a function of neuropsychological deficits and mode of stimulus problem presentation.

Koscinski and Gast (1993) recommend mastery of basic on mathematics as the stepping-stone to further achievements. Traditionally too, the efficient and automatic retrieval of the basic facts from memory was the mathematical goal (Fleischner et al., 1982). The prevalence of disability in arithmetics projected by Kosc (1974) is as much as six per cent of the school age population. Haward and Orlansky (1986) report of 5 to 30 per cent of the school age population with disabilities in arithmetics.

Kosc (1974) traces hereditary or congenital affliction of the brain substrate in mathematical function, this disorder clearly distinguished from other forms of disturbed mathematical abilities. According to Prased (1982), Joseph (1985) and Chalam (1996), children hailing from socially and educationally disadvantaged groups fail to achieve a minimum level of learning in mathematics and language. Lack of sufficient motivational factors for children at home and selective deficits in processes unique to calculation are quoted as reasons (Desai, 1985).

In economically deprived sections of society, the levels of medical and social pathology are high with profound effects on the child. Brief hospital admissions if repeated, can lead to educational failure especially in mathematics (Wolff, 1989).

Studies by Kirby and Becker (1988) demonstrate that the greatest numbers of arithmetic errors are due to the use of incorrect strategies or procedures. These incorrect procedures are characterized by the child selecting the wrong operation such as addition instead of subtraction or taking the wrong numbers away in subtraction. Other errors particularly when numbers larger than 10 are involved are due to conceptual difficulties regarding numbers (Resnick, 1983 and Russel and Gunsberg, 1984).

Deficiencies in mathematics among L.D. students emerge in the early years and continue throughout secondary school (Gakhar, 1986). Cawley and Miller (1989) report that the mathematics knowledge of students with learning disabilities tends to progress approximately one year for every two years of school attendance.

Mathematics has its own vocabulary, uses common words with a special meaning, employs complex concepts and involves string of relationships and making of generalizations thereby leading to more reading problems in mathematics than in any other subject content (Bond and Tucker, 1979).

As for gender issue in mathematics achievement, Harris and Liebert (1987) observe that in elementary school girls do about as well in mathematics as boys. In high school, boys out do girls by a considerable margin. The girls are more likely than boys to react to difficulties by feeling incompetent and giving up, whereas boys are more likely to react in mastery oriented way and work harder (Singh et al., 1994).

Eccler (1989) states that girls consistently had more confidence in their English ability than in mathematic skills. Parents of girls think that their children have to work harder in mathematics than parents of boys do, when teachers' think both groups can work equally hard. Problems in mathematics effect less confidence on the part of the poor achievers.

Share et al. (1988) investigated factors associated with reading disability and specific arithmetic disability in a longitudinal study of over 900 children assessed from age 3-13 years in New Zealand. Evidences revealed reverse patterns of strengths and weaknesses with regard to verbal and non-verbal skills, among boys but noticeably absent for girls.

Rourke (1993) summarizes the findings of the study focused on two groups of children aged (9-14 years and 7-8 years) with learning disabilities who exhibited equally impaired levels of arithmetic achievement but with different pattern of neuropsychological assets and deficits.

Sethia et al. (1994) conclude that the L.D. children despite beings slow, possess the ability and motivation to perform the task accurately, but are hampered by high cognitive load, which in turn requires slow and sustained effort. Numerous studies of Kirby and Becker (1988); Bhatia (1996) and Ramaa (1997) support the position that students with disabilities can be taught to improve their mathematical performance.

Loveland et al. (1990) compared 14 non-disabled control children with 13 L.D. impaired in reading and arithmetic skills and 12 children with learning disabilities in arithmetic but not reading. The results revealed that the L.D. had problems with social communication skills, the nature of the problem varying with the type of learning disability.

Mercer and Miller (1992) reveal that many students with deficiencies in mathematics exhibit characteristics that predispose them to math disabilities (eg. Problems in memory, language, reading, reasoning and metacognition). Their learning difficulties are often compounded by ineffective instruction. Shields (1989), Kelly et al (1990), Carmine (1991) and Babu (1996) believe that poor or traditional instruction is a primary cause for learning problems of many students in mathematics.

McIntosh et al. (1993) suggest effective integration of students with learning disabilities into the general education classroom. The L.D. children are capable of remarkable things. When trusted, they respond warmly with an understanding that is purely based on love which by itself proves to be a source of strength to draw from (Indra 1990).

(C) Arithmetic Competence Deficits and Its Impact

Learning of mathematical concepts is highly logical and abstract A mathematical concept is a mental construct acquired through abstracting a common response to the set of apparently different stimulus interaction.

Concept acquisition involves the process of associating understanding, based on real experiences and stimuli of the words

(Subramanyam, 1986). Hills (1993) Greenleaf et al. (1994) attribute difficulties in acquiring arithmetic competence to various influences both internal and external to the learner.

The results of a study by Light and Defries (1995) on assessment of genetic and environment etiologies leading to reading and mathematics deficits among 148 identical and 111 fraternal twin pairs aged 8 to 20 years suggest that about 20 per cent of the problem in reading deficits was due to genetic factors that influenced performance. Genetic and shared environmental influences appear to contribute almost equally to the observed covariance between reading and mathematics scores.

Approaching the problem from an empirical standpoint, Rourke (1993) and Rourke and Del Detto (1996) have identified two neuropsychologically distinct subtypes of arithmetic dysfunction. The first subtype occurred concomitantly with reading and spelling disorders. These children demonstrated intact visual, spatial and tactile perceptual skills. However, children in this group were deficient in their general, verbal and auditory perceptual abilities. The second sub-type was found to display normal achievement in areas other than arithmetic. Although this group demonstrated normal verbal and auditory perceptual skills, they were deficient on both visual, spatial and tactile perceptual measures (Batchelor et al. 1990).

Cawley et al. (1979) and Lovitt (1989) enumerated several factors leading to deficits in arithmetic as:

- Correlated failures - mathematics related to reading - children with difficulty in reading having problems in maths. Handwriting problems or difficulty in drawing simple shapes can negatively affect performance in maths. Difficulty in comprehending time, space, direction and quantity affect math abilities.
- Instructional failure - inappropriate instruction, incorrect or too limited exposure to develop the skill being taught.
- Shifted from one skill to another before reading competency.
- Tendency of the teacher to over correct, faulty and incorrect assessment of student performance.
- Faulty and incomplete assessment of student's performance.
- Individual failure - includes attention deficits, problems of encoding memory, organization and general disability in mathematics or dyscalculia.

Arithmetic achievement is correlated with a number of "non-intellective" variables including attitude, anxiety, interest, personality and teacher factors (Sumangala, 1995). At the same, these variables themselves necessarily interact with intelligence, verbal and spatial abilities. Normally intelligence is considered basic to success in mathematics, though its relative contribution depends upon individuals investigated and criterion measures employed.

Swedish studies on the psychological and social background of children have been based on cognitive learning theory. Faulty perceptions of concrete events representations of objects or events or abstractness were traced to be the factors associated with under achievement in maths (Magne, 1978).

Hitch and Mc Auley (1991) and Case et al. (1992) establish that students with learning disabilities demonstrated poor general mathematics achievement and were less adept at solving word problems than average or high achieving students. Most of the mistakes were not due to conceptual errors, instead executed the wrong algorithm and did not complete all the steps necessary to solve the problem (Kirby and Becker, 1988).

Mathematical disabilities in students include difficulties with psychomotor speed (Fleischner et al., 1987 and Kosinski and Gast, 1993), visual or auditory perceptual deficits (Lambardo and Drabman, 1985 and Hitch and McAuley, 1991, memory deficits (Bhatia, 1996), difficulties in developing automaticity by shifting from reconstructive (counting) to direct revival of strategies (Fleischner et el., 1987; Woodward and Haward, 1994).

Second and Vth graders with mild disabilities were monitored in reading and mathematics immediately before and after a summer vacation and six weeks into the following school year using Curriculum Based Measurement Probes by Allinder and Eicher (1994). The selected sample regressed significantly in both areas following the summer break. However, they regained proficiency in reading, but were performing at the same level in mathematics at the recoupment measurement time.

Seven, III grade children aged (8.5 to 9.0 years) with developmental dyscalculia examined by Shalve and Gross-Tsur (1993) attending mainstream classes had no academic progress. The authors suggest that the indicators for medical or neurological assessment be broadened to include children, not improving academically despite appropriate professional intervention.

Analysis of "think - aloud" procals by Case et al. (1992) revealed that L.D. students had more trouble than their normally achieving peers in identifying the needed information, understanding the problem and in organizing an efficient approach involved in problem solving.

Considering children with spatial difficulties but intact language abilities, Geary et al. (1987) are opinion that they might have difficulty keeping track of the object presented on the non-verbal problems, contributing to performance delays. However, the difficulties may become less important for calculation as children learn basic number facts.

Children with language difficulties but intact spatial abilities may perform at a normal level on non-verbal calculation problems but not on verbal calculation problems. In contrast, children with both language and spatial difficulties might perform below normal (Jordan et al., 1995).

Mathematics educators often stress on factors that interact with the learners' cognitive abilities as complexity of the subject matter, insufficient mastery of pre-requisite skills, motivational factors and inadequate instruction (Cawley et al., 1978).

Though structural learning is considered superior, Kirby and Becker (1988) suggest three cognitive factors responsible for children's learning problems in simple arithmetics as encoding of number, efficiency of operation execution and strategies for carrying out the operations.

In most individuals, the right hemisphere predominates for spatial and holistic processing, while the left hemisphere is specialized for analytic and logical aspects of both verbal and numerical function (Joshua, 1996). Problem solving and other complex forms of thought are believed to require fluency and integration of hemisphere functions (Jimenez, 1992; Kumar, 1995) characterized the roles of right and left hemisphere in arithmetic performance. Their respective roles as one or the other side of the brain are more influential during performance of arithmetic tasks.

Geary et al. (1995) identified three sub-types of early mathematical disabilities, two of which involved selected verbal processes. This classification scheme extended the earlier sub-typing work. The first sub-typing was characterized by difficulties in the representation and retrieval of arithmetic facts in semantic memory, the impairment associated with dysfunction involving posterior regions of the left hemisphere of the brain (Warrinton, 1982). Children of this category, had specific weakness in learning and in automatizing basic arithmetic facts even after extensive drill and practice in school.

The second sub-type involved difficulties with arithmetic procedures such as using counting strategies to solve calculation problems (Geary et al., 1987). Performance characteristics of procedural deficits included the use of developmentally immature arithmetic procedures, delays in acquiring basic procedural concepts and frequent errors in executing arithmetic procedures. Children with procedural deficits appeared to have general rather than specific diffculties with the acquisition of basic number concept. The third sub-type though not associated with verbal abilities is characterized by deficits in the spatial representation and interpretation of numerical information. The visiospatial sub-type involved dysfunction of the posterior regions of the right hemisphere of the brain (Venkataraman, 1996) and the children may have difficulty reading arithmetic signs.

Aiken (1972) proposed that mathematics itself is a specialized language. Mathematical language differs from ordinary language, thereby posing second language learning dilemma for children (Kumar, 1985 and Mercer and Miller, 1992). Children with language deficits may fail to solve word problems correctly even though they have competencies in calculations (Jitendra and Hoff, 1996).

Bhatia (1996) suggested that the same language difficulties that interfere with developing skill in reading also affect arithmetic performance, difficulties with arithmetic symbols or vocabulary and the language to organize and guide computational steps.

The importance of rich and meaningful vocabulary, knowledge in developing concepts is widely accepted by classroom teachers. Monroe and Panchyshyn (1995) justify difficulties with mathematics contending maths with more concepts per word, per sentence and per paragraph than any other area. Schiller and Rossano (1988) consider it particularly crucial to emphasize vocabulary instruction in mathematical content area. Calculation provides a foundation for later mathematical learning and it's difficulties can erode children's confidence in their mathematical abilities (Scary, 1990; Parmer and Cawley, 1991).

Jordan et al. (1995) reveal that children with different cognitive pattern may have different instructional needs in acquiring calculation skills. The use of verbal and non-verbal calculation tasks in educational assessment may prove to be helpful in characterizing young children's mathematical strengths and weaknesses.

In a related study among preschool, children Jordan et al., (1995) found that the non-verbal education tasks format is less sensitive to socio-economic variation than the verbal tasks formats. Children of low and middle-income families showed similar levels of performance on the non-verbal calculation task performing well below standard level. In contrast, children from low-income families performed much worse than middle-income children on story problems and number facts problems, because the former received less conventional verbal input at home (Kirk and Elkins, 1975). A follow up study one year later, showed that many of these difficulties persisted after formal instruction in the first grade (Jordan et al., 1995).

To sum up, it is apt to quote the expressions of Srinivasan (1994) that the "earlier the people are made to realize that mathematics is the "King of all Arts" and "Queen of all Sciences" and the earlier mathematics is considered and accepted as a creative subject of higher applicability, the better will be the quality of individual and social life".

(D) Remediation of Dyscalculic Children - Means and Methods

The major aim in diagnosing the disabled child is to determine the best remediation programme. Hence, the larger concept of assessment is a must to identify the problem and to determine the most beneficial types of intervention for the child with disabilities (Ramanujam, 1995).

Depending on the severity of the problem, remediation involves one (or more) of the following three hierarchical levels.

- Level A - focuses on age appropriate life tasks (basic knowledge, skills and interests)
- Level B - includes missing prerequisites for learning
- Level C - concerned with factors interfering with learning (disabilities, negative motivation and interfering behaviour).

In the past, majority of the programming for students with learning difficulties focused on language and reading, though currently large numbers of students with learning disabilities are receiving remediation in mathematics (Heward and Orlansky, 1988).

Assisting students with learning disabilities to learn mathematics more effectively requires a two step approach.

(a) Consideration of the disabilities that may contribute to difficulties in learning and

(b) Review of approaches, methods or strategies that appear to be valuable circumventing these disabilities (Starr, 1962 and Sewell, 1986).

Factors such as quantity taught, pacing, (fatigue and attention span) rate and mode of presentation (concrete objects, pictures or symbols) readiness or drill (sufficient understanding of the concept for repeated practice) level of interest and difficulty and lastly application in real life situations must be considered in developing remediation (Reisman and Kauffman, 1980; Kelly et al., 1990 and Vaidyanathan, 1995).

Prakash (1996) is of the view that the concepts taught in mathematics are superfluous, having no direct bearing on the children's day to day life. As a consequence, the ground reality is that a large number of them not only find it difficult to master the subject, but also struggle to cope with it.

As for teacher's efforts, Baker and Zigmond (1990) and observed that undifferentiated large group instruction was the norm with few accommodations made for students with individual differences. Jenkins et al. (1994) and Jaikumar (1997) consider grouping and supplementary instructions as the most enduring means of addressing ability differences, since no teacher can deny the importance and usefulness of individual guidance in learning. Kishore (1984) aims for mastery learning procedure - a special form of guidance in learning which allows a student learn at his own rate, providing continuous opportunity to check his learning.

For students with mathematical difficulties, Bond and Tucker (1979) and Jegathambal (1996) suggest an accurate command of all the technical symbols used as an important prerequisite without systematic instruction. Slow progress is made in acquiring sufficient skills to understand and manipulate symbols, abbreviations and numerals.

An attempt has been made in Table 1 to compile the studies on various remedial intervention methods used for children with learning difficulties in mathematics.

Table 1 : Remedial Intervention Methods for Dyscalculic Children

Method	*Procedures*	*Sample Size*	*Author*
Questions and answers in verbal problem solving	Questions used in seeking correct responces		Zweng et al. (1980) Fantasia (1981) Robertshaw (1981) Nazum and Morzola (1987)
Manipulative aids such as abacus, counting rods and paper clips	Positive evfects in overcoming subtraction problems		Lovitt et al. (1974)
Demonstration and Permanent modeling (D & PM)	Teach addition, subtraction and multiplication		Blackenship (1978) Sugi and Smith (1987) Meyer et al. (1992)
A Battery of Piagetion tasks	None advanced to concreate operation stage due to delay in transition Acquisition of reading skills was not dependent on the stage of operational development	Two - nine year old boys with normal IQ, language and reading ability	Sake and Shabeen (1981)

Method	*Procedures*	*Sample Size*	*Author*
Competency Based Instructional (CBI) Programme	Hierarchical order of specific concepts, attainment of one leading to next Breaking in to specific toals, terminal objectives and specification of activities.	1st and 2nd grades	Joshi (1983)
Strategy instruction and self instruct	Helpful in learning a new skill.		Leon and Pepe (1983) Glodman (1989)
Write and write and say	Used this method in mathematical problem solving		Lambado and Drabman (1986)
Verbalization for subtraction	Verbalisation for subtraction led to higher self-efficacy and skillful performance	LD 90 children aged 11 years 2 months to 16 years and 2 month grad 6-8	Schumk and Cox (1986)
True/False Reaction Time (RT)	Presented simple addition problems using time / false Reaction Time Tasks (RT) LD children required more time, had deficit in self monitoring and relied on counting strategy	77 Normal 46 LD from II, III and IV grade	Geary et al. (1987)

Method	*Procedures*	*Sample Size*	*Author*
Constant Time Delay method (CTD)	Provides systematic introduction of teachers: assistance in teaching multiplication facts.	2 boys, 3 girls	Gast et al. (1988)
Learner Responce Model-A Piagetian perspective	Teacher as facilitator provides a thorough basis for understanding space, number, seriation and classification.		Steven and Schuster (1988) Koscinski and Gast (1993) Gearheart and Gearheart (1989)
Token reinforces for correct response	Used for a structured set of mathematics problem in a two part experiment. Sample achieved 90% correct response against 34% correct response initially In the second part of the study, 100% correct response was achieved for multiplication and division.		Pavchinski et al. (1989)

Method	*Procedures*	*Sample Size*	*Author*
Use of concrete materials, pictures and symbols for multiplication	Flash cards and multiplication charts used helped. Casuarina rods materials and arithmetic blocks		Kurland (1990) Koscincki and Gast (1993)
Worksheets with Self Monitoring Checklists (SMC)	Included numeric device, 90 per cent level maintained 1-7 weeks after follow-up	2 groups of 3 students each	Brown and Frank (1990)
Strategy choice and Information Processing. Model (IPM)	Assessed the two methods in terms of difference among sample L.D. No. change, Group opted for frequent use of immature computational strategy and poor strategy choice	23 Normal 29 LD in maths I & II graders	Scary (1990)
Self paced computer based pattern recognition tasks	Inferential skills in problem solving and response to error examined. L.D. scored significantly lower than normal achievers	33 Normal 69 LD	Shafrir et al. (1990)

Method	Procedures	Sample Size	Author
Mediated transfer procedure and colour mediation procedure	Involved the association of each numeral with a colour. Number facts were rapidly learnt.		Van-Houeten and Rolider (1990)
Reinforcement, games, self instruction and calculators	Acquisition of facts such as addition, Subtraction and multiplication		Bakken and Scruggs (1991)
Extended remediation Learning sequences served as guides for remediation	Learning process elaborate on transition from concreate to symbolic to symbolic mode of doing arithmetics	Nine-second graders	Lopez (1991)
Token Reinforcement Congnitive Behaviour Modification (CBM) and Direct Instruction	Comparative study revealed significant differential gain between treatments and direct instructions. Groups to be equally effective through TR & CBM were superior to direct instruction.	94 LD students	Ross and Braden (1991)

Method	*Procedures*	*Sample Size*	*Author*
Simple self regulated strategy	Used in solving simple word problems.	Five elementary age students with LD	Case et al. (1992)
Concrete Semi-Concrete Abstract (CSA) teaching sequence	CSA sequence was an effective intervention requiring 3 to 7 lessons using manipulative devices/objects. Transfer of learning to abstract level made possible	7.7 to 11.3 years with disabilities in mathematics	Mercer and Miller (1992) Miller and Mercer (1993)
Modeling	Tasks requiring perceptual skills with or without model were used	50 LD boys with reading and mathematics deficits. 50 children without LD grade 3, 4 & 5. Age 8.5 to 12.7 years	Meyer et al. (1992)
Application of concepts to real life situations and mockshop	Results showed that children lacked understanding of place value, were unable to transfer it back to real life situations.	Among 25 children aged 6-12 years 15 children 7-17 years	Sutherland (1993)

Various remedial intervention methods tried out among dyscalculic children reveals the extent of research that has been effectively implemented in this specific area of mathematics.

According to Woodward and Howard (1994), errors though unavoidable elements in learning can be controlled and eventually eliminated through well-designed instruction, appropriate and immediate feedback, step by step instruction and efficient scheduling of newer different items.

Simple techniques suggested by Reisman and Kauffman (1980) and Brown and Frank (1990) include assigning fewer problems, minimizing or eliminating copying from the text book or blackboard, creative use of visual cueing (eg., collouring the steps), encouraging the use of finger tracing and using auditory cueing to reinforce visual input. Bartel (1982) recommends that teachers become familiar with the use of discovery method in teaching mathematics and the potential for flexibility in instructional approaches in planning.

It seems likely that major benefits would accrue from modifying current instructional practices to better match individual differences not only in developmental capability but also in motivation. The literature documented no doubt reveal that early diagnosis and remedial classes are a must with an understanding of the role of family, school, study skills, students' self-confidence identification and encouragement of talent. The new focus should be "catch them young" to prevent the developmental discrepancy and help them at risk category (Gopalakrishnan, 1992; Raghavan, 1996).

To sum up, as rightly pointed out by Narayanan (1994) and Silver and Hagin (1990) thoughtful consideration of organizational patterns in intervention models inevitably leads to the conclusion that there is no single structure or model that can be regarded as suitable for every child in the vast heterogeneous population of learning disorders. Though efforts have begun, a lot more needs to be done in this area in India.

Finding a learning disabled is easy according to Barsch (1992), but Bateman (1992) is of the idea that the difficult part is overcoming it. The key he says is the daily curriculum planned by the teachers. The final product of our endeavour must be a compact curriculum capsule, rich in simplicity and yet profound in complexity, which can be comfortably manned by a teacher.

It appears that one of the major challenges in remediation is to assure that a nurturing, self-enhancing, positive learning environment is maintained. Stimulation projects that enhance the learning process to a great extent be introduced. Making the education informal and interesting is the only way to encourage creativity among the learning disabled and enable them to overcome their problems.

(E) Teacher's Role-Tasks in Remediation

Teaching demands a range of skills and roles. The combinations of technical, organizational and interpersonal roles mean that teachers have to be exceptional people (Aludiapillai, 1993; Rao, 1994 and Sexena, 1994).

To quote Sri Aurobindo, "A good teacher is always a help in the pupils' pursuit of accomplishment and perfection". The teachers come into uplift the pupils efforts, knowledge and skills. A teacher's instruction, example and influence are the three instruments of good teacher orientation. According to Bras (1980), Rajaiah (1980), Appasamy (1996) and Joshua (1996) the attitude of the teacher will make a world of difference to a child's progress.

Singh (1996), Shamsuddin (1991) and Jayakumar (1997) proclaim that teacher education has been widened to include not only some professional skills, but also professional attitudes and values. The reasons put forth by Jangira (1990) for teachers not being able to meet the pedagogy of individual needs in the classroom are large class size, multi-grade teaching, heavy curriculum load, poor physical facilities and constraints of the system. Twenty million more primary teachers would be required in developing regions if the goal of Universal Primary Education is to be met by the year 2000 (ICCW, 1994).

The work of teachers is being acknowledged as one requiring cognitive processing. Teaching is not filling up of empty pails, but it is lighting of a fire. Teaching should lead to problem solving (Gopal, 1995) and the role of teacher is not being an instructor but be a facilitator (Bhasin, 1985, Gonsalvez, 1994 and Gupta,1996).

World Bank (1995) and Narayanan (1997) remark that teacher's knowledge is strongly and consistently related to student performance. Teachers with a wide repertoire of teaching skills are more effective than those with limited repertoire. The most effective strategy is ensuring that teachers have adequate subject knowledge and use instructional materials effectively (Singhal, 1997, Rao, 1996 and Sarojini Devi, 1997).

Falchikov (1993) and Muthukumaran (1995) envisage active student-centred, self-paced, self-discovery methods in education with a commitment to innovation and change on the part of the teacher. The National Policy on Education (1986) has also emphasized adoption of activity-based process of learning at the primary state (Chopra, 1991).

Bhasin (1985), Baksh (1996) and Emmanuel (1996) remark that the teaching-learning transactions will be impeded unless teachers understand the uniqueness of individual students and the general characteristics of children as learners (Mitchell, 1993).

Several studies on underachievement in sehad students have been conducted. These studies assess classroom advancement and do not attempt to identify the causative factors of these problems (John, 1995, Malavika, 1995). An attempt to identify these factors is essential for planning proper remedial programmes to such children and to create congenial classroom environment.Though remediation of some of these children requires specialized services, teachers have a major role to play in the management of most of these children (Kishore, 1984, Singhal, 1990). The major focus therefore should be to enable the teachers develop proper insight on the nature of learning disability (Jaya and Geetha, 1994). They must also try to match teaching strategies to pupils learning styles and their multi-dimensional personality (MacMay and Boyle, 1994).

Santhanam (1992) and Philip (1996) indicate that scholastic backwardness can be identified for appropriate referral by a sensitized teacher of the mainstream school through standardized yet informal assessment tool.

Ahuja (1995) pinpoints addressing learning disabilities through educational reforms. Gautam (1991), Khan (1995) and Rao (1997) consider that teacher's role is to inspire students for learning and act as a guide to impart certain skills, attitudes and competencies.

Teachers must know programmes best suited in terms of effective learning (Bhatia, 1996). Gearheart and Gearheart (1989) state that teachers of L.D. recognize disabilities assess them and provide remedial activities. Clegg (1972) and Katz (1993) observe that all children who find the learning process difficult need stable, affectionate, relationship with their teacher since the disability emerges due to anxieties, mental conflicts or deprivation during early childhood.

Daswani (1990) observes that if a teacher uses computer like the early teaching machines for tedious drill and practice, optimal use of this expensive technology will not be made. On the other hand, if such programmes are successful, they lower the drop out rate by 80 per cent and save teachers' time upto 90 per cent pupil enabling them to attend to the special needs of the individual learners.

Concerned with those who learn no more than what is in the prescribed text, Swaminathan (1994) and Kannayan (1997) opine that authorities who shape the curriculum and set standards for schools must pay attention to this serious drawback and devise ways appropriate to prepare the students better.

The teacher education scenario needs a thorough overhaul, deserving its due priority on the national agenda (Rajput, 1996). The implication of quality teaching for all according to Jangira (1990) and Gonsalvez (1994) is to ensure optimum learning by all children in the classroom despite the wide range of abilities due to interactive factors within the child, school, home and the community. This is possible when individual needs including special needs are met in the heterogeneous class.

With the advent of the education of the handicapped children gaining importance, various educational facilities are being experimented all over the world. The trend today is integrated education, leading to normalization. The philosophy behind this movement is that education provided in the least restrictive environment for the handicapped would minimize specialized provisions for community integration (Narayanan and Menon, 1989).

The National Council for Teacher Education, (NCTE), 1990 and Appasamy (1996) propose that teachers and schools should be prepared in a way that all children are able to learn to their fullest potential. Azad (1990) and Sacheendran (1996) forsee co-ordination of various agencies, Governmental and non-Governmental organizations discover ways and means to improve the methods of imparting special education. Another issue that special education has to address towards 2000 A.D. is the application of technology. Therefore- special education should gradually prepare itself for admitting the innovations in science and technology (Mani, 1986, Gupta, 1996). Implementing videodisc technology draws a dramatic change in the teacher's role from being an explainer to a manager of technology (Gersten and Kelly, 1992).

As Rao (1995) has rightly observed, "to improve the quality of cognitive and academic achievement in primary education the quality of teachers and instructional facilities should be improved". Akinaso (1993) and Kothari (1997) feel that investment in teacher training and appropriate instructional facilities would be worth while and teacher training and appropriate instructional facilities would be worth while and teachers have to change as the world is changing, for the children are far more alert, than they used to be (Fernandez, 1992, Pillowalla, 1993 and Kannappan, 1995).

The Teachers Education Resource pack developed by UNICEF is bound to hold the children in schools arresting high drop out rate bringing the goal of "Education for All" within reach in developing countries in a reasonable time frame (Jangira, 1991). The major challenge ahead lies in sustaining Universalisation of Primary Education (UPE) movement alive amongst the teaching community and the general public - till every child in the state is enrolled in primary schools and completes atleast five grades with minimum levels of learning. If the movement meets this challenge, it would be precursor of similar movement in other states as well (Govt, of India, 1993). The idea that we are educating the leaders of tomorrow demands rapid and effective training of teachers.

8

Methodology

The methodology for the present investigation on "Efficacy of Remedial Package in Augmenting Primary School Teachers' Skills to Help Dyscalculic Children", involved the following steps :

(A) Sensitizing Primary School Teachers on Learning Disabilities Among Children
(B) Identifying Dyscalculic Primary School Children
(C) Evolving Remedial Programme and Package for Dyscalculic Primary School Children and
(D) Evaluating the Efficacy of Remedial Package.

Figure 1: Reflects the research design in a nutshell.

(A) Sensitizing Primary School Teachers on Learning Disabilities Among Children

This phase included :

1. Getting to know teachers' awareness on learning disability
2. Organising sensitization programme for school teachers on learning disabilities and
3. Conducting an orientation programme for selected teachers

1. Getting to know teachers' awareness on learning disability

A survey among the local school teachers was found essential to assess their awareness on this relatively new dimension "Learning Disability".

PHASE I

SENSITIZING PRIMARY SCHOOL TEACHERS ON LEARNING DISABILITIES AMONG CHILDREN

- Assessing Teachers Awareness on Learning Disability
- Organising Sensitization Programme for Teachers
- Conducting Orientation Programme forSelected Teachers

PHASE II

IDENTIFYING DYSCALCULIC PRIMARY SCHOOL CHILDREN

- Assessing Academic Performance of Primary School Children
- Screening Low Achievers in Mathematics
- Identification of Children with Mathematical Difficulties

PHASE III

EVOLVING REMEDIAL PROGRAMME AND PACKAGE FOR DYSCALCULIC PRIMARY SCHOOL

- Developing Remedial Programme
- Using the Remedial Programme
- Evolving and Evaluating Remedial Package

Figure - 1 Design of the Study

This aspect of the study comprised the following steps.

(a) Selection of teachers

A list of Matriculation schools in Coimbatore Revenue District was obtained from the Directorate of Matriculation in the district, 30 schools located within the city comprised the sample unit for the present study.

The correspondents / principals / heads of selected school were explained the purpose of the study. Ensuring their co-operation, 150 teachers handling classes I to V were selected adopting the purposive sampling method.

(b) Preparation of a questionnaire

A questionnaire was prepared to elict information on teacher's background viz., age, educational qualification, experience, training programme attended and their awareness of the concept, types, causes, characteristics, identification, assessment and educational requirements for children with learning disabilities.

As stated by Kothari (1996) in a pilot study, the replica and rehearsal of the main survey brings to light the weaknesses in the tool. Hence, the questionnaire prepared was pretested for its suitability among 10 school teachers.

Appendix I gives the finalized questionnaire used for data collection.

(c) Collection of teachers' responses on issues related to learning disability

The selected teachers were explained the purpose of the study. The questionnaires were then distributed and collected from the teachers for further analysis.

2. Organising sensitization programme for school teachers on learning disabilities

The responses of selected teachers to the questionnaire brought to light the need to educate and inform them on the concept of learning disability. Almost 80 per cent of the teachers were found to be quite ignorant of its prevalence, meaning and implications. This finding necessitated organizing a one-day sensitization programme on "Dyslexia Among Primary School Children".

A list of primary schools (Aided / unaided / and private Matriculation) obtained from the office of the Chief Educational Officer, Coimbatore was used. Permission was also sought for deputation of teachers for the programme.

An invitation informing the schools of the theme, guest speakers, date, time and venue along with a brief write up on the concept of learning disabilities (Dylexia) among young children and the need for equipping the teachers on this concept was dispatched to the head of institutions three weeks in advance for their perusal and for circulation among the staff.

Appendix II The sensitization programme attended by 130 participants included primary teachers (47) secondary grade teachers (53), principals / correspondent (18), special educators, specialists and university teachers (12). (Plate I)

Plate 1 Sensitization Programme for Teachers

Appendix III gives the details of the programme, topics discussed, resource persons invited and the questionnaire used in assessing the teacher's awareness on learning disabilities prior to the sensitization programme.

3. Conducting an orientation programme for selected teachers

Implementing this programme involved the following tasks:

(a) Planning for an orientation programme

An orientation programme on "Identification and Education of Learning Disabled Children", was planned for five days in the Department of Human Development. Appendix IV gives an overviews of the programme.

Invitations were sent to all the 30 Matriculation schools selected for the study and through personal visits, efforts were made to enroll as many teachers as possible to participate in the programme. Nineteen primary school teachers attended the five day programme organized in collaboration with Madras Dyslexia Association, Madras.

The major focus of the programme was on discussing and clarifying the concept and educational issues related to learning disabilities among school going children.

(b) Evolving instructional materials on learning disabilities

As teachers were found less competent on the issues related to learning disability and had limited access to reading materials efforts were made by the investigator to develop "Instructional Materials" aimed at providing the teachers an understanding of learning disabilities in a comprehensive manner. This involved :

(i) Developing and refining the instructional materials

Related literature on learning disabilities from various sources like books, journals, magazines and manuals from libraries of various universities and institutions, namely (Madras Dyslexia Association, Madras, Alpha to Omega Learning Centre, Madras and National Institute for the Mentally Handicapped (NIMH) Hyderabad aided in the preparation of the instructional materials.

(ii) Validating content of the prepared materials

The literature collected was scrutinized and thoroughly analyzed to make the presentation of materials simple, clear and precise. In the process, the need for suitable, easy to comprehend instructional materials was realized. Taking into cognizance this aspect, the following materials were prepared:

- Leaflet - Concept of learning disability
- Booklet - Specific learning disabilities - Terminology and identifiable errors
- Pamphlet - Causes of learning disabilities
- Flip book - Problems of the learning disabled
- Folders - Characteristics of learning disabled children and

- Teaching methods for specific learning disabilities

A checklist on selected parameters for evaluation viz., clarity, flow of thought, handiness, informativeness and simplicity was prepared (Appendix V) to check the adequacy and appropriateness of the developed instructional materials. The checklists were distributed to five experts each in the fields of Education (2) Human Development / Special Education (2) and Psychology (1). As per their recommendations, necessary modifications were incorporated. The final manuscripts thus prepared were distributed to the participating teachers in the programme for use. Instructional materials prepared as part of this study are included in the remedial package.

(c) Conducting and assessing the programme

The main aim in organizing the orientation programme was to introduce primary school teachers to the concept of learning disability among young childern and to make them operationally effective in their class rooms and publicize the fact that most children irrespective of the degree of severity of learning disability can be remediated and be helped.

Extensive use of the instructional materials developed was a salient feature of the programme. Dissemination of information during the programme was made through talks by experts, group discussions and individual assignment (Plate II).

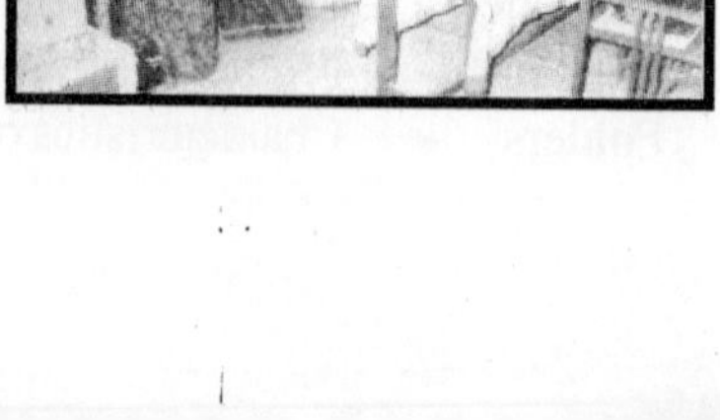

Plate 2 Orientation Programme in Action

Evaluation is defined as systematic effort to determine the worth of a programme or some intervention effort (Wolf, 1986).

Evaluation of the orientation progamme was done by assessing knowledge acquired by the teachers on learning disabilities before and after their participation in the five day programme.

(B) Identifying Dyscalculic Primary School Children

This part of the study probed into the following aspects :

1. Assessing academic performance of primary school children
2. Screening low achievers in mathematics and
3. Identification of children with mathematical difficulties (dyscalculics).

1. Assessing academic performance of primary school children

In order to know the scholastic performance of primary school children in their learning environment, an overview of their academic achievement for an academic year was found necessary.

Five matriculation schools that had evinced keen interest in the conduct of the present investigation were considered for the collection of data. From the records maintained in school, the marks of students from classes I to V during the academic year (1994-95) were recorded.

Among the five schools selected, three were co-educational and one each had boys only and the other exclusively girls. For uniformity, only four major subject areas viz., English Language, Mathematics and Science were considered and the average marks in five tests were obtained to analyze the general academic performance of students.

2. Screening low achievers in mathematics

This feature of the study involved :

(a) Confirming disability in mathematics

Based on teachers' opinion and the achievement of students in mathematics from classes I to V in four consecutive tests (I midterm, quarterly, II midterm and Half yearly) for the academic year1995-96, students scoring less than 40 per cent on an average were identified. Thus a total of 115 students in the age range 6 to 11 years were pinned down as low achievers in mathematics from the five matriculation schools considered.

The present investigation necessitated the use of the following tools in order to confirm the disability in among the 115 low achievers in mathematics.

(i) Raven's Coloured Progressive Matrices (RCPM)

The Coloured Progressive Matrices development by Raven (1985) is used satisfactorily with people who for any reason have difficulties in perception. Rao (1988) and Ramaa (1993) report that RCPM is internally consistent and homogeneous for young children.

This test is a non-verbal, untimed power test for children under 11 years. The RCMP consists of 36 coloured multiple-choice materials (3 sets, A, AB, B each with 12 problems). Each subset of RCPM is designed to measure different aspects of general ability i.e., set A "the apprehension of discrete figures as spatially related wholes" and set B "both apprehension of analogous change in spatially and logically related figures". The problems in different sets are arranged in such a way to assess the cognitive processes of children.

Limited data exist, however, on the differential performance characteristics of students classified as learning disabled. As Parmar et al. (1994) contends that the learning disabled group have IQ scores in the range of normal ability on Raven's. Hence, to assess the intellectual ability of the selected low achievers in Mathematics (N=115) Raven's Coloured Progressive Matrices test was administered.

(ii) Arithmetic diagnostic test for primary school children

The above test developed and standardized by Ramaa (1994) diagnosis specific difficulties in arithmetics encountered by primary school children. The test covers the major areas viz., number concept, arithmetic process operations (addition, subtraction, multiplication and division) and arithmetic reasoning (assessed at different levels through word problems and other types of problems dealing with the judicious application of the fundamental arithmetic operations in solving them) Appendix VI.

Since it is a diagnostic test, it includes sums that represent each type and subtype of tasks that fall under each of the three major areas. Two items in the case of arithmetic process and reasoning represent each subtype of the task. This helps in thorough diagnosis of the difficulties faced by the children in dealing with particular subtype of arithmetic tasks. The sub-items and items are arranged in order of increasing difficulty level within the different sections of sums as well as between the sections.

(iii) Behavioural checklist for screening the learning disabled (BCSLD)

Research on L.D. children has identified a variety of attentional deficits (Ramaa, 1992 and NCERT, 1997). The children exhibit behavioural characteristics, which make them disruptive in the classroom and at home (Rao, 1988). Hence, the tool developed and standardized by Swarup and Mehta (1991) was used to assess the behavioural characteristics of the selected children.

The behavioural checklist consists of 30 items-positive and negative to be filled by the teacher. The eight areas assessed using the BCSLD include : deficits in visual processing, auditory processing, motor coordination cognitive domain, language, memory, preservation tendencies and disorders in affective domain (Appendix VII).

(b) Collection and analysis of data

The above aspect involved :

Step 1: Administration of intelligence test

All the selected 115 children from classes I to V were administered the Raven's Progressive Matrices Test. The test was administered individually and scoring was done as per instructions in the manual. On the basis of scores obtained on this test, selected children were classified into five grades.

Grade (I) or "intellectually superior", if his / her score lies at or / above the 95th percentile for people of his / her age group.

(II) "definitely above average" in intellectual capacity, if his/ her score lies at or above the 75th percentile.

(III) "definitely average" he / her score is greater than the median or 50th percentile.

(IV) if his / her score is less than the median.

(V) "definitely below average" in intellectual capacity, if his/ her score lies at or below the 25th percentile.

(IV) . If his/ her score lies at or below the 10th percentile and

(V) "intellectually defective", if his / her score lies at or below the 5th percentile for his / her age group.

In the above classification, a slight modification was done to suit the present study. Children whose percentile points fell in between 25th and 10th percentile were also considered as children with average intelligence, since some of the non-dyscalculic children had also scored below the 25th percentile.

Step 2: Administration of arithmetic diagnostic test

This test was administered to all selected 115 children in groups of five in two sessions of 60 minutes duration each. For children in classes I and II only number concept, addition and subtraction sums were given in the first session and for those in classes III, IV and V number concept, addition and subtraction sums were given in the first session and multiplication and division sums were presented in the second session.

To find out the strengths and weaknesses of the children with reference to different types of arithmetic tasks, their performance was qualitatively analysed in terms of the tasks that they were capable of doing and those not successful.

Step 3: Administration of the behavioural checklist for screening the learning disabled.

The behaviour checklist was given to the class teachers of selected children with guidance to fill in for the individual student and it was collected back after one week.

For the negative items in the checklist the weightage given was as follows : Yes - 2, No - 0 and ? - 1. For the positive items Yes - 0, No - 2, and ? - 1. The maximum obtainable score is 60.

3. Identification of children with mathematics disabilities

Among the 115 children from classes I to V earlier identified as low achievers in Mathematics and screened for mathematical performance, 63 childrem were short listed as probable dyscalculics on the basis of various tests administered.

Among the 63 children identified, 27 children were eliminated on grounds of subnormal intelligence, underage and absence of any associated behavioural problems. Finally only 36 children were found to be having arithmetic disabilities.

Further, an attempt was made to establish difficulty in neuropsychological areas among the 18 identified dyscalculic children (experimental group) using Diagnostic Test for Learning Disability standardized and developed by Swarup and Mehta (1992), (Appendix IX).

From the school records, consultation with the class teacher and observations by the investigator, the identified children (36) were found to be normal in visual and auditory performance, were provided with the required schooling and were encouraged by parents in their educational pursuits. Thus these children fulfilled all the criteria to identify them as children with arthmetic disabilities (dyscalculic) for the purpose of the present investigation.

C) Evolving Remedial Programme and Package for Dyscalculic Primary School Children

This aspect of the study involved :

1. Framing remedial programme for identified children
2. Using the developed remedial programme and
3. Evolving remedial package for children with mathematical disabilities

. Framing remedial programme for identified children

To integrate and implement remedial programme for the selected children with mathematical disabilities, they had to be grouped based on age, class and level of difficulty.

Among the 36 children identified, only 18 children (Experimental group) were considered for remediation on the basis of accessibility and co-operation extended by the schools. The remediation took place in two groups as under :

Group A - Nine children 5 girls and 4 boys in the age group 6-8 years who had scored less than 30 per cent in the pretest and were observed to have made maximum errors in counting, addition, subtraction and writing numerals in words and numbers

Group B - Nine children of 8-10 years (5 girls and 4 boys) 40 per cent in the pretest with errors in verbal problems, subtraction, multiplication and division.

The remaining 18 children served as control group.

On identifying the areas of difficulty in the various mathematical concepts learnt by the children in the classroom, an attempt was made to use various teaching aids while introducing multiple intervention strategies.The remedial programme was developed incorporating multi-sensory approach to inculcate the required skills with the following objectives.

- Teach mathematical concepts identified as difficult
- Provide continuous exercises in the conceptual area until mastery.

2. Using the remedial programme developed

Teachers handling mathematics from the respective schools were oriented towards using and implementing the developed programme. The investigator co-ordinated in working with the teachers for effective implementation of the programme.

Since concentration was laid only on the acquisition of particular computation skills, a minimum of 20 sittings and maximum of 30 sittings of 90 minutes duration for remediation was found adequate for each child.

Plate 3 Remedial Intervention in Operation

To help the students acquire practice and mastery of the various skills for increasing their rate of computation "time bound probes" were administered during remediation to enable them to gain adequate skill and confidence with the computational facts (Plate III).

In order to evaluate the acquisition of basic skills taught during remediation, a post-test using the same diagnostic tool as in pre-test was administered.

3. Evolving remedial package for children with mathematical disabilities (dyscalculics)

The investigator's experiences on working among children with mathematical disabilities resulted in the preparation of a remedial package for primary school teachers for use with children having difficulties in mathematical computation.

It was observed that students with deficiencies in mathematics had social and emotional problems. In school settings, mathematics problems often resulted in school failures that led to high levels of anxiety. Bartel (1982) and Kulak (1993) state that students with mathematics deficiencies are as disabled as individuals with reading problems, as daily living requires the application of mathematical skills.

The fact that most of the students go in for special mathematics intruction pins down the importance of providing effective instruction for students with mathematical difficulties. It has been observed by Radhakrishnan (1996) that difficulties with numerical relationship can begin at an early age.

The challenge therefore lies in identifying the skill deficits and in improving instruction for these students using the remedial package.

In this study, the remedial programme was developed on undertaking a thorough analysis of the existing curriculum in the primary schools. The main components in the package included concept of learning disabilities, information on number instruction, uses of manipulative aids and resource materials (Plate IV) specific strategies in mathematics instruction, project activities and games (Appendix X).

The major input in the remedial programme was adoption of multi sensory approach wherein the basic concepts of addition, subtraction, multiplication, and division were taught to the selected group.

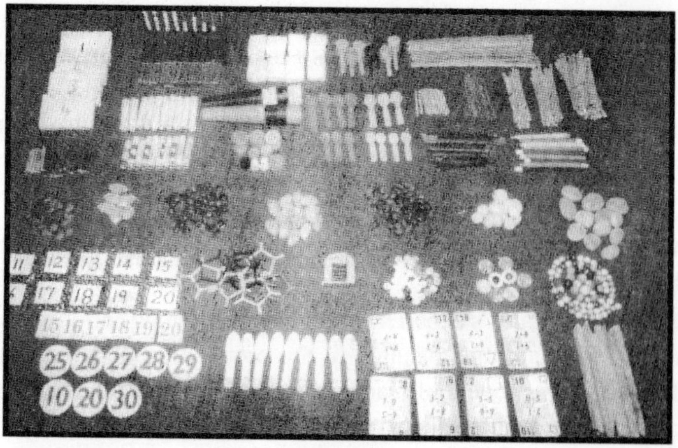

Plate 4 Manipulative aids and Resources Materials used

(D) Evaluating the Efficacy of Remedial Package

The remedial package developed was then evaluated by distributing the same to ten primary school teachers handling mathematics two from each of the five schools selected. A checklist was evolved to test the efficacy of the same (Appendix XI).

Data thus obtained in the conduct of the various aspects of this investigation were analysed and discussed in Chapter IV.

9

Results and Discussion

The findings of the study on **"Efficacy of Remedial Package in Augmenting Primary School Teachers' Skills To Help Dyscalculic Children"**, are discussed under the following major heads:

(A) Awareness of Primary School Teachers on Learning Disability Among Children

(B) Identifying Dyscalculic Primary School Children

(C) Remedial Intervention for Dyscalculic Children

(D) Efficacy of Remedial Package for Dyscalculic Children

(A) Awareness of Primary School Teachers on Learning Disability Among Children

This aspect of the study discusses:

1. General profile of selected teachers
2. Teachers' awareness of learning disabilities among children
3. Evaluation of sensitization programme for school teachers on learning disability and
4. Outcomes of orientation organized for school teachers

1. General profile of selected teachers

One hundred and fifty primary school teachers (women) from 30 Matriculation schools within Coimbatore city were selected for the present investigation. Questionnaires distributed to the selected teachers broughtforth information presented below:

The general information on primary school teachers included age, educational qualification, teaching experience, number of classes handled, students strength and training programmes attended by them are indicated in Table 2 given below:

Table 2: Profile of Selected Primary School Teachers

Aspects	*Teacher's stating (N=150)* Number	*Percentage*
Age (in years)		
20-30	69	46
31-40	64	43
41-50 and above	17	11
Educational qualification		
Graduation with B.Ed. and M.Ed.	97	66
Post Graduation with B.Ed. and M.Ed.	43	29
Diploma in education	10	7
Teaching experience (in years)		
2-4	79	53
4-8	71	47
Number of classes handled		
1-2	34	23
2-4	62	41
4-6	54	36
Students strength per class		
10-30	28	19
31-60	107	71
61-70	15	10
Programmes attended		
Subject related seminars	25	17
Child development seminars	3	2
Montessori training programme	2	1
Seminar on slow learners	1	0.7
Preschool education	1	0.7
Nil	118	79

Forty six and 43 per cent of the selected teachers were in the age range of 20-30 years 31-40 years respectively. Those above 40 years were 11 per cent. Among the teachers, 65 per cent were graduates followed by 29 per cent post graduates.

It is the experience that adds to the efficiency of the teacher. In this study, 53 per cent had 2-4 years of teaching experience followed by 47 per cent with 4-8 years in teaching primary school children.

The number of classes handled by a single teacher ranged from one to six. Two to four classes were handled by 41 per cent of the teacher. Almost 36 per cent of the teachers handled 4-6 classes reflecting the heavy work load on a single teacher at the primary school level.

Information on students' strength in the classes revealed that 19 per cent of the teachers had less than 30 students per class, 71 per cent had 31-60 students and 10 per cent had a strength of almost 70 students in their classes.

Opportunities for the primary school teachers to attend enriching programmes were found to be rather very limited in that only two per cent of the teachers had attended seminars on child development followed by less than two per cent attending Montessori training programme. Seventeen per cent of the teachers attended individual subject related seminars in English, Science, Mathematics and Poetry. Seventy nine per cent of them had no exposure to any such programmes. This reveals the dire need for organizing in-service training programmes for these teachers to equip them with the latest developments in the field of education of young children.

2. Teachers' awareness of learning disabilities among children

Awareness of selected teachers on learning disabilities among school children as elicited from their responses are presented below:

(a) Learning Disability - Concept

Table 3 and Figure 2 provide perceptions of the selected teachers' terminology of learning disability.

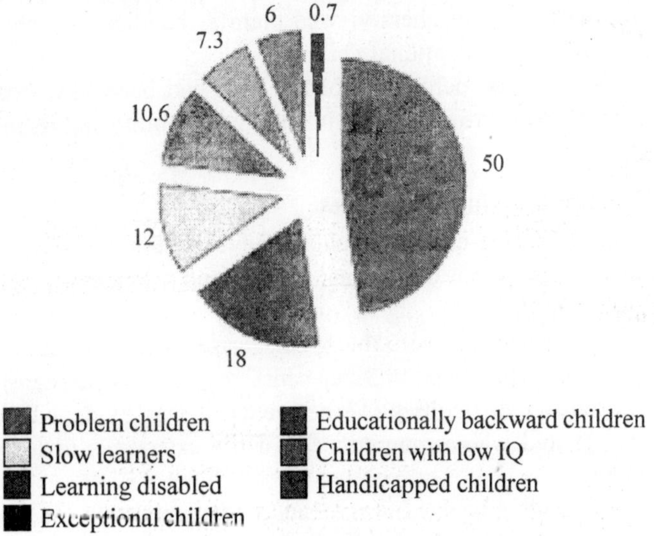

Figure 2
Learning Disability as Perceived by Selected Teachers

Table 3: Learning Disability as Perceived by Selected Teachers

Perceptions	*Teacher's stating*	
	Number	*Percentage*
Problem children	75	50
Educationally backward children	28	19
Slow learners	18	12
Children with low IQ	16	11
Learning disabled	11	7
Handicapped exceptional children	9	6

Multiple Response

Among the various terminologies used in referring to children with learning problems, 50 per cent of the teachers perceived them as 'problem children' in their classrooms, while 19 per cent referred them as 'educationally backward' and 12 per cent as 'slow learners'. Nearly 11 per cent of the teachers presumed them to be children with low IQ.

With no basic training inputs in this emerging field, only seven per cent teachers branded them as children with learning disabilities though no assessment was done for the diagnosis of the problem. Six per cent of the teachers viewed them as handicapped children referred them as 'exceptional children'.

The teachers' perception of the L.D. had been low, because they had no exposure or training in learning disability and its related issues.

(b) Specific learning disabilities

Micro-level researches conducted have identified specific learning disabilities as that of reading, writing and arithmetic disability (Sarangi, 1989).

Selected teachers were able to categorize these children as those with writing difficulties (19.3 per cent), reading (18 per cent) and with arithmetic difficulties (13 per cent). It was evident that the teachers lacked wholesome concept of the categories of learning disabilities.

This finding brings out the need to incorporate a module on children with learning disabilities into curriculum at all levels of the teacher training programmes. Perhaps, the need to orient the teacher trainees cannot be undermined anymore.

(c) Causes

Table 4 depicts the awareness of teachers in relation to causes of learning disability among school children.

Table 4: Causes of Learning Disability as Viewed by Teachers

Causes	*Teacher stating (N=150)*	
	Number	*Percentage*
Poor teaching in school	54	36
Lack of early stimulation	39	26
Lack of awareness on causes	14	9
Discouragement by parents	9	6

One of the major reason assigned by 36 per cent of teachers as the cause leading to learning disability was poor coaching (inadequate instruction) prevailing in schools with respect to individual learners. This is in accordance with Taylor and Sternberg (1989) and Devi (1996) who are also of the view that environmental situations outside the child in the form of inappropriate instruction and lack of reinforcement are the causes for learning disability.

Fernandez (1992) considered decreased parental and environmental stimulation as the factors for increased risk of learning disabilities. In the present investigation, only 26 per cent of the teachers attributed lack of early stimulation as a factor responsible for learning disabilities.

Lack of awareness on causes among teachers (9%) and discouragement of children by parents in case of academic failure (6%) were also some of the causes stated by the teachers.

(d) Characteristics

The characteristics of L.D. children in relation to the problems experienced by the teacher in the classroom are listed in Table 5 and given in Figure 3.

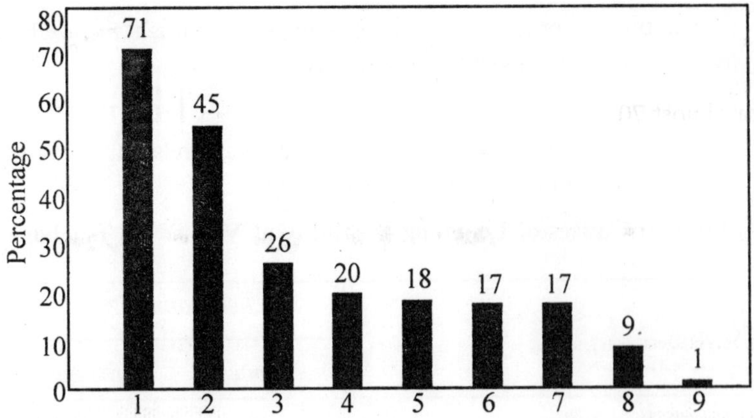

1. Behaviour problems
2. Lack of concentration
3. Lack of memory
4. Distractibility
5. Language problems
6. Social withdrawal
7. Poor self concept
8. Academic failure
9. Dependency behaviour

Figure-3

Characteristics of Learning Disabled as Perceived By Teachers

Table 5: Characteristics of Learning Disabled as Perceived by Teachers

Characteristics	*Teacher stating (N=150)*	
	Number	*Percentage*
Behavioural problems	107	71
Lack of concentration	67	45
Lack of memory	39	26
Distractability	30	20
Language problem	27	18
Social withdrawal	26	17
Poor self-concept	25	17
Academic failure	14	9
Dependency behaviour	2	1

As Alexander et al. (1993) considered behavioural difficulties in youngsters with learning problems as a significant concern, majority of the selected teachers (71 per cent) highlighted the associated behavioural problems among the L.D. children as a significant characteristic, followed by 45 per cent stating lack of concentration. The other characteristics mentioned included lack of memory (26%), distractibility (20%), language problems (18%), social withdrawal (17%), poor self concept (16%), academic failure (9%) and dependency (1%).

The responses of the teachers pin down the fact that in order to determine the degree of learning disability among the primary school children, there arises a need to orient the in-service teachers on the nature and characteristics of L.D. children.

(e) Tools for identification

From the listed options in the questionnaire, 66 per cent of the teachers felt that informal classroom tests and observation could be easily adopted for identification of L. D. children. In the words of Taylor (1989) observation is an important tool to detect student problems at an early stage. It was encouraging to note that 63 per cent of the teachers favoured use of checklist for identification.

Since children with learning disabilities have observable behaviour problems, 46 per cent and 28 per cent of the teachers expressed that behavioural assessment and study of home environment respectively could also be used to identify children with learning problems. Medical examination for identification of children with learning difficulties was reported by few teacher (6%).

(f) Teaching considerations

Table 6 depicts teachers' awareness of teaching considerations for the learning disabled.

Table 6: Teaching Considerations for the Learning Disabled

Teaching considerations	*Teachers stating (N=150)*	
	Number	*Percentage*
Goals setting	56	37.3
Individual variations	43	28.6
Mainstreaming	40	26.7
Special educational needs	38	25.3
Referral support	34	22.7
Personal skills	22	14.6
Teaching procedure	9	6.0

Goal setting for an individual learner as an important pre-requisite in the teaching process was considered important by 37 per cent of the selected teachers. Only 29 per cent of them were aware of the individual variation in the degree of learning to be considered as an important factor in planning individual educational plans for the L.D. children.

On the other hand, 27 per cent of the teachers had been aware of the possibilities of integrating mild L.D. with normal children. While 25 per cent teachers considered special education needs as basis for their curriculum planning, use of referral support available for L.D. was mentioned by 23 per cent. Apparently only 15 per cent had understood the need for being equipped with skills for communication. Verbal explanations followed by demonstration were the teaching procedures mentioned by a few teachers (6%).

The low awareness of teachers on learning disabilities among school children reflects the urgent need to build in and to equip them with the required knowledge, since they are responsible for the education and management of children they are also in a position to remediate children with learning disabilities and contribute towards "Education for All".

Obviously, it is realized that regular classoom teachers are inadequately prepared to educate and mainstream children with learning disabilities. As NCERT (1995) reports, it is important that teachers, administrators and related service personnel, who are instrumental for improvement of school performance of the children, be trained. Therefore, effective school reform must include provisions to enable practicing teachers to review and refine their professional skills in the area of learning disability.

3. Evaluation of sensitization programme for school teachers on learning disability

A sensitization programme organized on learning disability attended by 130 participants, included secondary grade teachers (53), primary teachers (47), principals and correspondents (18) and special educators, specialists and university teachers (12).

Among the participants, a majority of 38 per cent belonged to the age group 21-30 years and 33 per cent to 31-40 years. In the age group 41-50 years, there were 19 participants and only nine per cent were 51 years and above. An analysis of their qualification revealed that there were 29 per cent female and five per cent male graduates, while among the post graduate category there were 19 per cent female and 14 per cent male participants.

All the participants knew about the programme only from the invitations dispatched to the heads of institution and for almost 70 per cent of the participants, it was their first programme on this concept. Less than one per cent made a mention of their participation in selected in-service training programmes, National Council for Educational Research and Training (NCERT) and State Council for Education Research and Training (SCERT) workshops relating to educational procedures and those organized by UNESCO for primary school teachers.

Among the participating teachers, 97 per cent were definite about the prevalence of learning disabilities among the children.

The various categories of specific learning difficulties observed among children by the teachers are enlisted in Table 7 and Figure 4.

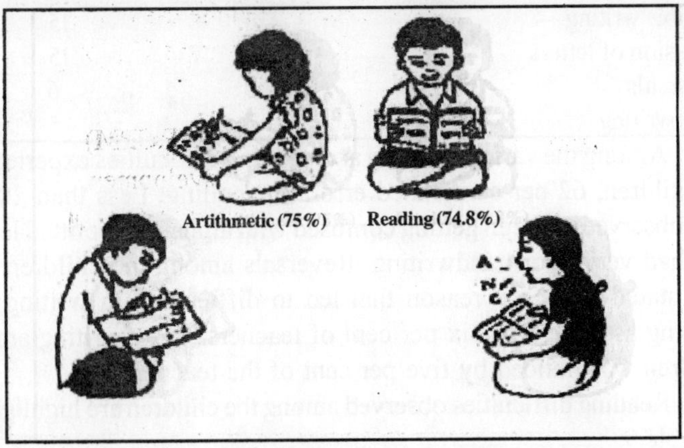

Figure 4 Learing Difficulties Among Children as Observed by Teachers

Table 7: Learning Disabilities Observed Among Children by Teachers

Specific area	*Teachers stating*	
	Number	*Percentage*
Writing	102	78.4
Arithmetic	98	75.3
Reading	96	73.8
Spelling	93	71.5

Poor handwriting was a persistent problem observed by 78 per cent of the participating teachers followed by difficulties in arithmetic (75%), reading (74%) and spelling (72%). Though no specific tools had been used by the teachers for identification, they were able to spot out 1176 (boys) and 1269 (girls) with learning difficulties.

Some of the very common errors committed by young children in writing as well as in spelling as perceived by the teachers are focused in Table 8.

Table 8 : Specific Writing and Spelling Difficulties Observed Among Children by Teachers

Difficulties	*Teachers stating*	
	Number	*Percentage*
Spelling errors	81	62
Confusion of letters	25	19
Illegible writing	20	15
Omission of letters	13	15
Reversals	8	6
Slow writing	7	5

Among the various writing and spelling difficulties experienced by children, 62 per cent stated errors in spelling. Less than 20 per cent observed children getting confused with alphabets, omitted letters - and had very poor handwriting. Reversals among the children was also stated to be the reason that led to difficulties in writing and spelling as opined by six per cent of teachers. Slow writing among children was noticed by five per cent of the teachers.

Reading difficulties observed among the children are highlighted in Table 9.

Table 9: Difficulties in Reading Among Children

Difficulties	*Teaching stating*	
	Number	*Percentage*
Mispronunciation	77	59
Slow in reading	25	19
Grammar comprehension	11	8
Fast reading without comprehension	9	7
Omission of words	5	4
Fear of reading	4	3

In the perception of teachers, prominent reading difficulty among children included mispronunciation of words (59%) and slow reading (19%) less than 10 per cent of the teachers stated problems in comprehending grammer and fast reading without comprehension of facts as learning difficulties experienced by the students.

Less than five per cent of teachers indicated omission of words and fear of reading among children.

Learning problems in mathematics have traditionally received less attention than those in other academic areas eventhough children do experience a wide range of difficulties in the same.

Table 10 and Figure 5 reflect reasons behind the errors made by the children in mathematics.

Table 10: Reasons for Errors in Mathematics

Reasons	*Teachers stating*	
	Number	*Percentage*
Carelessness	50	38
Poor understanding of concepts	29	22
Poor number concept	24	18
Difficulties in division	19	15
Difficulty in memorizing tables	14	11
Poor concentration	14	11
Errors in symbols	8	6
Misplacing digits	8	6
Forgetting formulas	7	5
Errors in fundamental operations	7	5

Little more than one third of the teachers (38%) attributed errors in arithmetic to carelessness among young children. Poor understanding of the basic concepts and their differentiation including that of number concept stood next in the list, having been noticed by 22 per cent and 18 per cent of teachers.

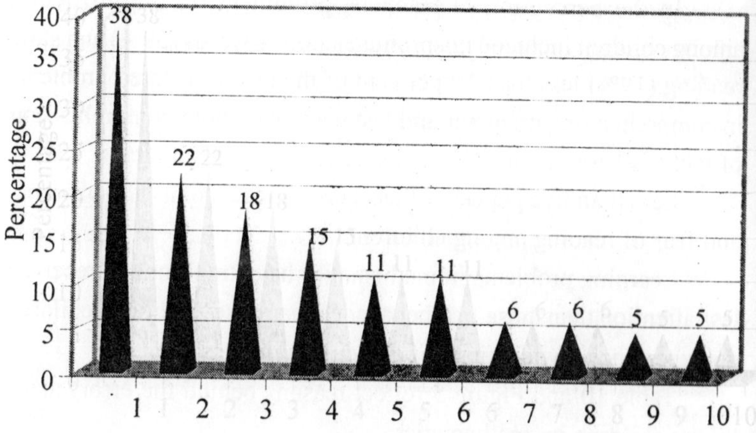

1. Carelessness
2. Poor understanding of concepts
3. Poor number concept
4. Difficulties in division
5. Memorizing table
6. Poor concentration
7. Errors in symbols
8. Misplacing digits
9. Forgetting formulas
10. Errors in fundamental operations

Figure 5 Reasons for Errors in Mathematics as Perceived by Teachers

Difficulty in doing division sums, in memorizing tables, poor concentration, errors in use of symbols, place value and in working with fundamental operations and formulas were reported by less than 15 per cent teachers.

Some of the common methods adopted by the teachers in helping children with learning difficulties are indicated in the Table 11 below.

Table 11 : Methods Adopted by the Teacher in Helping Children with Learning Disability

Methods	*Teachers stating*	
	Number	*Percentage*
Motivation	99	76
Special attention	95	73
Extra coaching	86	66
Parental involvement	51	39
Use of teaching aids	50	38
Recognition of abilities	49	38

Table 12 : Knowledge Scores of Teachers on the Concept and Causes of Learning Disability

Concept	*Pre-test*		*Post-test*		*Difference in Mean ± S.D.*	*Period 't' value*
	Percentage (N=19)	*Knowledge scores mean ± S.D.*	*Percentage (N=19)*	*Knowledge scores mean ± S.D.*		
Terminology - Learning disability	26.3	0.26 ± 0.44	100	1 ± 0	0.74 ± 0.45	6.76**
Mean percentage	26.3		100			
Specific learning disability						
Reading disability	47.3		100			
Writing disability	15.7	0.21 ± 0.52	100	1 ± 1.41	0.79 ± 0.74	4.48**
Arithmetic disability	-		100			
Mean percentage	21.0		100			
Causes						
Poor teaching in school	52.7		94.7			
Lack of attendence among parents and teachers	52.7		100			5.37**
Heredity	-			0.89 ± 1.57	0.63 ± 0.51	5.37**
Illness of mother during pregnancy	-	0.26 ± 0.55	78.2			
Mean percentage	26.3		89.4			

** P<0.05

It was encouraging to note that though none of the teachers had any formal training in helping children with learning difficulties, almost 76 per cent of them had adopted the techniques of motivating these children to learn better and improve. Amidst their heavy work load, 73 per cent of the teachers were able to render special attention and 66 per cent were even able to spend a few extra hours to coach and guide the children in their problem areas.

Request for parental involvement in helping the child at home, use of teaching aids and focussing the children's abilities were some of the methods adopted by less than 40 per cent of teachers. Though the number practicing is less, these methods tend to have a far-reaching impact on the minds of the children to cope with their difficulties.

4. Outcomes of orientation organized by the school teachers

Nineteen teachers participated in the orientation programme of five day duration. Initial and final assessment of knowledge (in terms of knowledge scores) was taken to assess the impact of the orientation programme. Paired 't' test applied to test the difference between the pre and post mean knowledge scores and the outcomes are presented below :

(a) Concept of learning disability

Table 12 depicts pre and post-test knowledge scores of teachers assessed for learning disability concept, categories and cause for learning disability among children.

Prior to orientation programme, the teachers referred to the children as "handicapped", "exceptional", "problem children" and "children with low IQ". Pre-test data further revealed that the terminology "learning disability" had been referred to by only 26 per cent of the teachers. After the orientation all the teachers revealed a better understanding of this terminology. Significant difference at five per cent level between pre and post mean knowledge scores on concept of learning disability is an encouraging positive outcomes.

As for specific learning disabilities, it was quite surprising to note that none of the teachers in the group were aware of arithmetic disability among school children, while reading and writing disability were known to 47 and 16 per cent teachers respectively.

On the contrary, after the training, all the teachers had comprehended well the three different types of learning disabilities, the difference between pre and post mean knowledge scores being significant at one per cent level. This finding forecasts an immediate need to orient all the teachers on specific learning disabilities, so that children with such problems can be given timely and appropriate help.

Prior to the orientation programme, 53 per cent of the teachers opined poor teaching (inadequate instruction) and lack of awareness among parents and teachers as factors leading to learning disabilities against 95 per cent and the difference was significant statistically after the orientation. Apparently this orientation programme had offered an opportunity for about 81 per cent of the teachers to gain knowledge on the significance of hereditary factors and illness of the mother during pregnancy, as contributive sources to learning disabilities.

Characteristics

Table 13 lists manifestations of learning disabilities reported by teachers at pre and post training levels.

The characteristics of the learning disabled listed by the teachers included lack of concentration and language problems (42%), motors problems (37%), poor self-concept and social-withdrawal (32 %) and memory problems (26%). Over dependency and disruptive behaviour were mentioned by very few teachers (5%). None of the teachers were aware of the distinguishing features like repeated academic failure due to learning difficulties in the areas of reading, writing and arithmetic, impulsivity, distractability and difficulty in following oral directions prior to their participation in the orientation programme. The percentage of teachers pointing to the above characteristics increased significantly after the orientation programme.

In the pre-test, teachers mentioning the various characteristics ranged from five to 42 per cent as against 84 to 100 per cent in the post-test. In the orientation programme, the teachers (84 to 100%) obviously had good focus on the last four characteristics in Table viz., academic learning difficulty (100%), impulsivity (95%), distractability (84%) and difficulty in following oral directions about which they were totally ignorant initially. Majority of the teachers gaining perception of the characteristics and its associated problems as indicators for the learning disability of the child appears to be a favourable outcome of the orientation programme and was proved statistically too.

Table 13 : Knowledge Scores of Teachers on the Concept and Cause of Learning Disability

Characteristics	*Pre-test*		*Post-test*		*Difference in*	*Period 't'*
	Percentage (N=19)	*Knowledge scores mean ± S.D.*	*Percentage (N=19)*	*Knowledge scores mean ± S.D.*	*Mean ± S.D.*	*value*
Lack of concentration	42.1		100			
Language problems	42.1		84.2			
Motor problems	36.8		100			
Poor self-concept	31.5		100			
Social withdrawal	31.5	0.81 ± 0.15	89.4	0.92 ± 3.07	0.74 ± 1.28	2.51*
Memory problems	26.3		94.7			
Over dependency	5.26		94.7			
Disruptive behavior	5.26		84.2			
Academic learning difficulty	-		100			
Impulsivity	-		94.7			
Distractability	-		84.2			
Difficulty in following oral directions	-		84.2			
Mean percentage	18.4		92.5			

* $P<0.05$

(c) Tools for identification

Table 14 shows teachers' comprehension of the tools used for identification of children with learning disabilities.

It was quite encouraging to note that in the pre-test level, 58 per cent teachers were aware of both formal and informal assessment tools such as classroom test and observation, followed by 42 and 26 per cent of the teachers comprehending the use of behavioural assessment and checklist respectively for identification of learning difficulties.

A substantial and significant increase in both the number stating and knowledge scores related to tools used were recorded in the responses of teachers in post-test level depicting greater understanding of the same on the part of the teachers.

Remedial methods

Teachers' awareness on the remedial options for L.D. Children in a classroom situation under pre and post-test condition is projected in Table 15 and Figure 6.

As for remedial options for the L.D., 50 per cent of the teachers were aware of the multi-sensory approaches in teaching followed by coaching by specially trained teachers (47%). Individualized instruction (37%) and peer tutoring (26%) were also stated. It was rather surprising to note that none of the teachers knew about the functioning of the remedial centers for L.D. children in the metropolis prior to their participation in the programme. It was quite encouraging to observe that the orientation programme had enabled the teachers to acquire information on the programmes and functioning of the remedial training centres both within the state and outside.

Remedial services in terms of individualized instruction, peer tutoring and functioning of dyslexic training centers had limited spread among the teachers in the pre-test (0 - 58 %), while the post-test brought forth as much as 66 to 99 per cent and difference in scores was significant at five per cent level.

(B) Identifying Dyscalculic Primary School Children

The second phase of the study involving identification of dyscalculic primary school children included the following steps:

1. Academic achievement of primary school children
2. Low achievers in mathematics - an overview
3. Identification of dyscalculic children and
4. Dyscalculic children -their distribution

Table 14 : Knowledge Scores of Teachers on Tools for Identification of Learning Disabled

Tools	*Pre-test*		*Post-test*		*Difference in Mean ± S.D.*	*Period 't' value*
	Percentage (N=19)	*Knowledge scores mean ± S.D.*	*Percentage (N=19)*	*Knowledge scores mean ± S.D.*		
Formal / informal assessment tools	57.8		100			
Behavioural assessment	42.1	0.42 ± 0.64	94.7	0.96 ± 1.37	0.54 ± 0.50	4.69**
Checklists	26.3	94.7				
Mean percentage	42.1		95.5			

** P<0.01

Table 15 : Knowledge Scores of Teachers on Remedial Methods for Learning Disabled

Concept	*Pre-test*		*Post-test*		*Difference in Mean ± S.D.*	*Period 't' value*
	Percentage (N=19)	*Knowledge scores mean ± S.D.*	*Percentage (N=19)*	*Knowledge scores mean ± S.D.*		
Multi-sensory approach	57		90			
Trained special teacher	47.3		85			
Training behavioural assessment	37	0.33 ± 0.70	85	0.81 ± 1.64	0.48 ± 0.83	2.51*
Peer tutoring	26		79			
Remedial centres	0		66			
Mean percentage	33		81			

* $P<0.05$

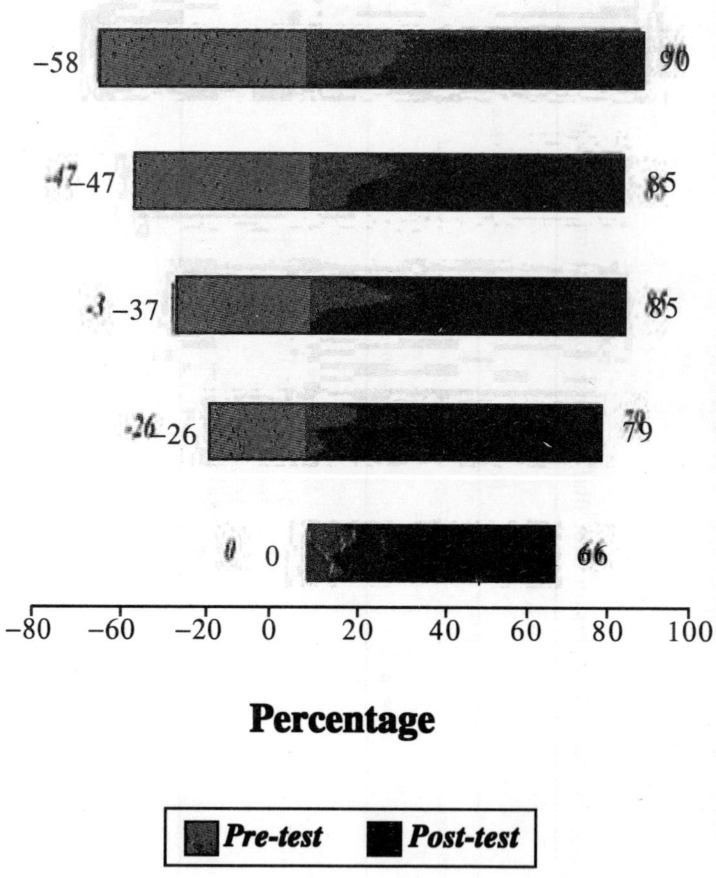

Figure 6
Knowledge Scores of Teachers on Remedial Methods for Learning Disabled

1. Academic achievement of primary school children

As a prelude to the identification of dyscalculic primary school children the investigator made an attempt to assess the overall academic performance of primary school (1442) in four major subject areas of English, Language, Mathematics and Science over a period of one academic year.

Chi-square test was applied to find the association between academic scores in various subject and gender. The analysis revealed significant association between academic score and gender at 1 % level for English, Science and Mathematics only $x^2 = 40.15, 53.19, 17.48$).

Table 16 depicts the performance of children in mathematics in relation to other subjects.

Table 16: Performance of Children in Mathematics in Relation to Other Subjects

Subject	*Sex*	*Score*	*Group sample in subjects*	*Group sample in maths*	*CR*
	Girls-	Below 40	53	66	1.238
		40-80	508	480	1.433
		Above 80	244	259	0.807
English					
	Boys-	Below 40	71	77	0.525
		40-80	441	398	2.541*
		Above 80	125	162	2.481*
	Girls-	Below 40	127	66	4.680**
		40-80	472	480	0.406
		Above 80	206	259	2.914**
Language					
	Boys-	Below 40	77	77	0.000
		40-80	366	398	1.830
		Above 80	194	162	1.998*
	Girls -	Below 40	61	66	0.462
		40-80	503	480	1.176
		Above 80	241	259	0.969
Science					
	Boys-	Below 40	99	77	1.786
		40-80	388	398	0.576*
		Above 80	150	162	0.782*

* P<0.05   ** P<0.01

A Proportion test (P test) was applied to find out whether the proportion of girls and boys who had secured below 40 in English, Language and Science were the same. The test revealed significant difference at 1 % level in the case of language only among girls.

Even though the selected group of children showed poor performance in language predominating other subjects, performance in Mathematics was considered because there is a strong evidence cited by Crealock and Kronick (1993) that students with learning disabilities are usually first identified because of their reading problems, the correlation between reading and mathematics being high for many students since both are language - one primarily qualitative and other quantitative.

2. Low achievers in mathematics - an overview

Low achievers in mathematics were identified by the teachers on the basis of their class performance and also by an assessment of their marks scored in the three tests (viz., first mind-term, quarterly and half-yearly). Thus from the selected five schools a total of 115 children were identified to be poor achievers in mathematics.

The family background details of the selected children are discussed below:

(a) Low achievers - class-wise and sex-wise

The class-wise and sex-wise distribution of low achievers in mathematics is given in Table 17.

Table 17: Distribution of Selected Children Class and Sex-wise

Class	*Distribution of children (N-36)*				
	Boys		*Girls*		*Total*
	Number	*Percentage*	*Number*	*Percentage*	*Percentage*
I	14	12	1	1	13
II	12	10	4	4	14
III	22	19	5	4	23
IV	26	23	2	2	24
V	13	11	16	14	25

An increasing trend was observed in the percentage of low achievers in mathematics class-wise. Among the selected children, only 13 per cent were in class I while almost 25 per cent were identified at class V. This brings out the fact that the higher the class, greater is the number of primary school children with difficulties in mathematics.

Sex-wise distribution of low achievers in mathematics revealed a majority of 87 children out of 115, were boys and only 28 were girls.

(b) Educational Qualification of Parents

Table 18 depicts educational qualification of the parents of selected children.

Table 18: Educational Qualification of Parents

Educational qualification	*Distribution of children (N=36)*			
	Father		*Mother*	
	Number	*Percentage*	*Number*	*Percentage*
Primary education	10	9	17	15
Secondary education	70	61	72	63
Higher Secondary	16	14	15	13
Graduates	13	11	9	7
Post graduate	2	2	0	0
Others (Diploma certificate course)	4	3	2	2

A majority of almost 60 per cent of both parents were educated only up to the secondary level. Around 14 per cent of the parents were either graduates or had completed their higher secondary grade level. Less than five per cent of the parents were diploma holders in computer education, technical education or textile technology. It was noticed that only two per cent of the fathers were post graduates.

A significantly greater number of low achievers in mathematics had fathers at low professional level, low income and lower educational levels. This was also true of children whose mothers had lower levels of education (Nair, 1981). This finding relates well with the observations of Grolink and Slowiaczek (1994) that parental education has positive effect on children's achievement in mathematics.

(c) Occupational status

Considering the occupational status it was noticed that low achievers' mothers, to a large extent, were housewives (90%) while the remaining were engaged as either teachers, agents, or in business owning a beauty parlour or a laundry.

Seventy three per cent of the fathers of low achievers were engaged in business / trades such a cotton, gold smithy, workshops etc. around 22 per cent of them were in other occupations like salesman, telephone operators, document writer, compositor, driver, time 'keepers, commission agents, dhobi etc. a few among the fathers were teachers (4%) or held professional jobs (2%).

(d) Family income

Table 19 reveals the total family income per month.

Table 19 : Total Family Income per Month

Income range	*Distribution of Children (N=115)*	
	Number	*Percentage*
Low income group (Rs. 1,250 - 2,650)	65	57
Middle income group (Rs. 2,650 - 4,450)	37	32
Middle income group (Rs. 4,450 - Above)	13	11

* (HUDCO, 1994)

The analysis revealed that a majority of 57 per cent of children were from low income group, while 32 per cent were from middle income and 11 per cent were earning a monthly income of above Rs. 4,450/- to a maximum of Rs. 15,000/- and thus belonged to the high income group.

In addition to the income of parents, education, ordinal position and occupation of mothers were the demographic factors that affected academic performance significantly (Desai, 1990).

3. Identification of dyscalculic children

Identification of dyscalculic children among the 115 identified low achievers in mathematics involved diagnosis in the following areas:

(a) Assessment of performance in mathematics

Table 20 percents the average marks obtained by selected children in mathematics in four consecutive tests.

Table 20 : Performance of Selected Children in Mathematics

Marks range	*Distribution of Children (N=115)*	
	Number	*Percentage*
0-10	6	5
11-20	44	38
21-30	48	42
31-40	17	15

Marks in mathematics from four tests (1st mid-term, quarterly, II mid-term and half yearly exam.) were considered to arrive at the average score obtained by these selected children.

An average of less than 30 marks in mathematics had been scored by 42 per cent children, while 15 per cent scored an average of less than 40 per cent marks.

A totally discouraging performance was observed among 38 per cent children who had scored less than 20 marks. Five per cent of them had scored even less than 10 marks on an average. This group of children were probably children with difficulties in mathematics requiring assistance through appropriate remediation.

(b) Intelligence test

The scores obtained by the selected children in different grades on the Raven's Progressive Coloured Matrices is presented in Table 21.

Table 21 : Grade-wise Classification of Children on Intelligence Test .

Grade	*Classification*	*Distribution of Children (N=115)*	
		Number	*Percentage*
I	Intellectually superior	-	-
II	Deficiency above average	4	4
III	Average	39	34
IV	Deficiency below average	47	41
V	Intellectually defective	25	22

Since the selected group of children included poor achievers in mathematics, it was not surprising to observe than one of them belonged to Grade I classified as 'intellectually superior' (95th percentile points). Only four per cent of children belonged to Grade II, classified as "above average" in intelligence, their percentile score being 75th percentile point.

Thirty four per cent of children belonged to "average intelligence" group. In Grade IV category "definitely below average" in intelligence, 41 per cent children were grouped. Thus children with average and above average intelligence and with failure in basic arithmetic skills, in the Arithmetic Diagnostic Test administered were assumed to the dyscalculics.

(C) Behaviour problems

Sharma (1993) and Yasodhara (1996) contend that undiagnosed learning problems lead to explosive outbursts of frustration among young children and dyscalculic children might manifest behaviour problems.

Behaviour problems among the selected children were recorded using behavioural checklist for screening the L.D. developed by Swarup and Mehta (1992). Table 22 reveals the number of children with and without behaviour problems among the 115 low achievers in mathematics.

Table 22: Prevalence of Behaviour Problems Among Selected Children

Criteria	*Distribution of Children (N=115)*	
	Number	*Percentage*
Children		
With behaviour problem	94	82
Without behaviour problem	21	18

The behaviour assessment made by the class teachers revealed that a majority of 82 per cent of the selected low achievers exhibited behaviour problems as per the norm. Obviously 18 per cent of children had no behaviour problems. Probably the children with behaviour problem may manifest learning difficulties.

(d) Responses of children while doing arithmetic test

Arithmetic diagnostic test for primary school children and standardized by Ramaa (1994) was administered to all the low achievers in mathematics. The responses of these children towards the test are given in Table 23 and Figure 7.

Table 23: Responses of Children Towards Arithmetic Diagnostic Test

Responses	*Children (N= 115)*	
	Number	*Percentage*
Failure in basic arithmetic skills	63	55
Inconsistent responses	22	19
Difficulty in higher order tasks	20	17
Incomplete without obvious reason	6	5
Failure to perform lower order tasks (though capable of higher order ones)	4	4

A large number of 63 children (55%) had problems in basic arithmetic skills and were most likely to be dyscalculics, therefore these children were short listed for further assessment and diagnosis. Inconsistent responses were observed among 19 per cent of children and 17 per cent of them had difficulty in higher order mathematics tasks. Few children (6%) showed incomplete responses and failure to perform lower order tasks even though capable of handling higher order ones. Thus the children's strengths and weakness in solving problems in various concept areas in mathematics could be identified.

This analysis show a direction to think that children with difficulty in basic arithmetic skills tend to continue with their problems though they get promoted to higher classes with marks for a minimum pass based on their performance over the academic year.

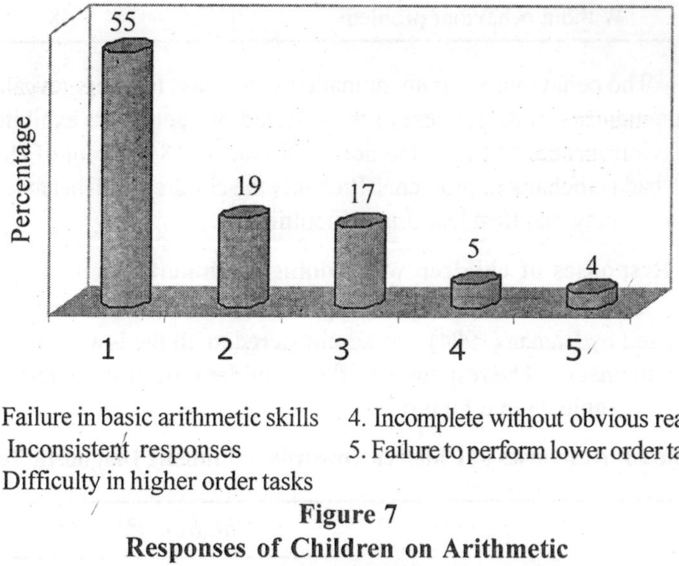

1. Failure in basic arithmetic skills
2. Inconsistent responses
3. Difficulty in higher order tasks
4. Incomplete without obvious reason
5. Failure to perform lower order tasks

Figure 7
Responses of Children on Arithmetic Diagnostic Test

(e) Confirming dyscalculia among children

The process of identification of probable dyscalculics involved a step-wise diagnosis. Table 24 below gives a glimpse of the diagnostic criteria followed to confirm dyscalculia among the selected children.

Table 24 : Identification of Dyscalculic Children

Criteria	*Number of children (N=115)*	
	Eliminated	*Retained*
Arithmetic diagnostic test	52	63
Subnormal intelligence	18	45
Underage	2	43
Children without behaviour problem	7	36

Out of 63 children identified as probable dyscalculics on the basis of their difficulty in doing basic arithmetic skills, a total of 27 children were eliminated since they were under age, had subnormal intelligence and had no behaviour problems.

Thus the exclusion procedure followed led to the final children 36 confirmed as dyscalculics.

(f) Dyscalculic children - their distribution

On confirming dyscalculia among selected children, an attempt was made to trace their class and sex as in Table 25 Figure 8.

Table 25 : Dyscalculics - class and sex-wise distribution

Class	Distribution of children (N=36)				
	Boys		*Girls*		*Total*
	Number	*Percentage*	*Number*	*Percentage*	*Percentage*
I	6	17	0	0	17
II	2	6	1	3	8
III	10	28	3	8	36
IV	8	22	2	6	28
V	2	6	2	6	11

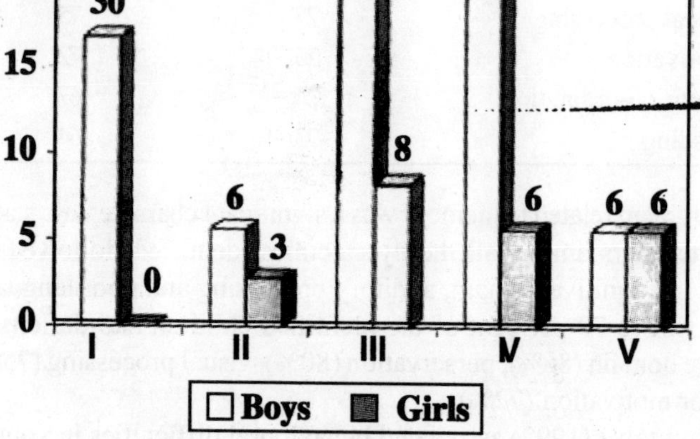

Figure 8
Class and Sexwise Distribution of Dyscalculic Children

Out of the 36 identified dyscalculics, a majority of 78 per cent were boys and the remaining 22 per cent were girls. Class-wise, 36 per cent were from class III followed by class IV (28%) class (17%) V (11%) and class II (8%).

Though an increasing trend of poor achievers was observed grade-wise in mathematics performance in the ascending order, the number of dyscalculics grade wise did not reveal a similar trend.

(g) Deficits among dyscalculics

Table 26 depics some of the behavioural deficits exhibited by the identified dyscalculic children.

Table 26 : Deficits Exhibited by Dyscalculics in Selected Areas

Problem areas	*Distribution of children*	
	Number	*Percentage*
Deficits in		
Memory	36	100
Auditory processing	34	94
Cognitive domain	34	94
Language	34	94
Affective domain	31	86
Preservation	29	80
Visual processing	27	75
Motivation	26	72
Motor co-ordination	24	67
Reading	23	64

Problem related to memory was a significant characteristic stated by the teachers among all the dyscalculics identified, followed by deficits in cognitive domain, auditory processing and poor language (94%). Above 70 per cent of the identified children had deficits in affective domain (86%), perservation (80%), visual processing (75%) and poor motivation (72%).

Kowsalya (1992) associated behavioural difficulties in youngsters with learning problems as a significant concern. True to this finding, all children in the present study also exhibited associated behaviour problems characteristic of L.D. children.

(h) Type of errors committed

An analysis of arithmetic errors committed by the identified dyscalculic children on the Arithmetic Diagnostic Test is revealed in Table 27.

Table 27 : Arithmetic Errors Committed by Identified Dyscalculics

Types	*Distribution of children (N=36)*		
	Example	*Number*	*Percentage*
Cannot perform multiplication	7 x 3 = ?	20	56
Random response	23+14=90	19	53
Writing the number said	Six hundred Seventy As 60070	15	42
Wrong operation	Adding in between subtraction	14	39
Understands concept but cannot do it in written symbolic form	Problem solving	14	39
Reading digitwise	1006 as one, zero, zero six	13	36
Spelling errors	hundred-hundred	10	28
Lack of knowledge of carryover	87+44=1211	8	22
Reverses two place numbers	14 becomes 40	7	19
Substracting lower number from higher numbers irrespective of the place value	72 - 45 = 33	6	17
Reversing the digits	21 becomes 12	6	17
	61 becomes 16	4	11
Rotation of numbers	2 - 7	1	3
Counting by fingers		1	3
Cannot subtract		1	3

Almost a little above 50 per cent of children had difficulty in committing multiplication tables to memory and also attempted in random responses. The other category of errors included writing the number mentioned (42%), wrong operation and errors in verbal problem solving, difficulty with written symbolic form (39%), reading digit-wise (36%) and spelling errors (28%).

Less than three per cent of the sample committed errors related to rotation of numbers and counting by fingers in problem solving. The overall performance of three children that finally emerged out of the analysis of errors committed was that a majority of dyscalculics did face difficulty in understanding and remembering the rules that govern different mathematical operations.

This finding supports the conclusion drawn by Ramaa (1992) that dyscalculics at the primary level have the above mentioned types of errors. Crealock and Kronick (1993) found that L.D. youngsters do not readily use organized strategies that facilities memorization and recall. These students have difficulty in mathematics because they fail to use cognitive strategies in computation or problem solving. This report also confirms the above observation.

1. Performance of dyscalculic children on diagnostic test of learning disability

An analysis of the strengths and weaknesses in the various neuropsychological process areas among dyscalculics selected for remediation is shown in Table 28.

Table 28 : Strengths and Weaknesses of Dyscalculics in the Neuropsychological Process Areas

Areas	*Number of children scoring (N=18)*		
	(Maximum score = 10)		
	Below 4	*4 - 8*	*8 and above*
Memory	11	5	-
Expressive language	9	4	-
Receptive language	6	8	2
Cognitive abilities	5	10	1
Eye hand co-ordination	3	11	2
Position in space	2	9	5
Figure ground perception	2	12	2
Auditory perception	2	14	-
Spatial relations	1	14	1
Figure consistency	-	10	6

As for the performance of dyscalculics in the individual neuropsychological areas, it was noticed that they had severe problems in the areas of memory (11), expressive language (9), receptive language (96) and cognitive abilities (5). The abilities of the dyscalculic children in the areas of figure ground perception, figure consistency, position in space in eye hand co-ordination were relatively good.

(j) Prevalence ratio

Ramaa (1994) identified 15 dyscalculic children out of 251 cases, thus establishing a prevalence of dyscalculia to an extent of six per cent in the population studied. The present investigation reveals the percentage of dyscalculic to be 2.5 per cent among a total of 1442 children. Such an alarming proportion calls for immediate efforts on the part of educators to overcome the situation, which might take bigger dimensions, if left unattended.

These findings typify the need for orientation to equip the primary school teachers to handle children with difficulties in learning especially in mathematics. Kavanagh and Truss (1988) and Radhakrishnan (1996) contend that problems in mathematics achievement may be directly related to faulty instruction and uninteresting classroom environment. Thus it is recommended that teachers need to undergo courses in individualized remedial mathematics teaching to gain in-depth focus on dyscalculia and its related features among children.

Children who fail in primary grades or those not able to cope with basic subject such as mathematics might drop out. While all our efforts are being taken to establish 'Education for All' 31 per cent dyscalculics cannot be neglected and allowed to miss their education. Hence, it is imperative that primary school teachers are trained in the multiple perspectives of learning disabilities and be equipped to help young children gain proper foundation.

(C) Remedial Intervention for Dyscalculic Children

This aspect of the study had two basic objectives:

(a) To plan remedial programme for the dyscalculic children grouped A and B

(b) To study the effectiveness of the remedial programme in improving the accuracy of solving mathematical problems with minimum errors.

(a) Remedial Intervention

The remedial programme for the selected experimental group children (18) grouped A and B for the convenience of remediation was implemented using sample programmes given in Appendix X. Remediation was offered to the groups by the teachers who had offered to be the resource teachers along with the investigator in implementing the programme in the respective schools.

The basic five modalities considered in planning and implementing the remedial programme involved.

- The present mode in which the students were shown the pictures or pictorial activity sheets.
- The construct mode in which the manipulative resource materials were used (stacked, arranged, sorted, grouped, etc.).
- The oral mode in which oral discusions / oral instructions / communication took place.
- The graphic symbolic mode in which written or oral symbols were used.
- The identity mode in which non-verbal response by actual use of working on point was done.

With these input and output options, a variety of instructor - learner interactions were planned allowing the teachers to select alternative learning combinations for students. These multiple options enabled to circumvent difficulties among these children in other areas such as reading and writing that may impede mathematical performance.

In order to make the treatment uniform to all dyscalculics intervention was provided in terms of extra coaching at home or in schools excepting the remedial intervention.

(b) Evaluation

The effectiveness of the remedial programme was done by evaluating the students' scores on the Arithmetic Diagnostic Test implemented.

Table 29 depicts the percentage scores of the two groups (experimental and control) in the pre and post-test.

Table 29 : Performance of Selected Children on Arithmetic Diagnostic Test

Group	*Mean*	*Standard deviation*	*'t' value*
Control	Pre-test 17.42	6.9	12.51**
	Post-test 33.12	7.32	
Experimental	Pre-test 33.21	14.69	9.28**
	Post-test 64.37	11.81	

** $P<0.01$

Paired 't' test applied to find out the difference between the control group (pre and post-test) scores and experimental group (pre and post-test) scores revealed significant difference in their performance in Arithmetic Diagnostic Test. Obviously after the remedial intervention, the performance of the experimental group improved with a mean value 33.16 against the control group mean 15.70 on the Arithmetic Diagnostic Test.

(D) Efficacy of Remedial Package for Dyscalculic Children

Working with the teachers in the schools in providing remedial intervention for dyscalculic children brought to light that the teachers do not possess the required knowledge and skills in managing children with learning difficulties in mathematics in the classroom. Seemingly the literature available in this area is also limited in India. Hence, there is a need to enrich and expand the scope and availability of such materials. Therefore, an attempt was made by the investigator in developing a remedial package for children with difficulties in arithmetics - an additional supplement to the already available literature in India.

The package developed was distributed to ten primary school teachers (including resource teachers who had helped in remediation) to obtain their views on the efficacy of the package for use by teachers in classroom interventions.

A checklist was provided to get teachers' opinion on the use of the package. Table 30 depicts the opinion of the teachers on remedial package.

Table 30: Teachers' Views on Efficacy of the Remedial Package

Aspects	*Percentage of teachers stating (N=10)*
Remedial programme largely applicable	100
Manipulative resource materials provide imaginative learning	100
Mathematical skills can be improved	98
Simple method in concept learning useful	99
Games provide interesting learning situations	97
Adequate computation skills can be taught	95
Objectives of remedial teaching achieved	89
Instructional materials on the concept is informative	85
Parents and teachers can use the package without orientation	85

It was quite encouraging to note that all the teachers expressed that the remedial intervention spelt out in detail was largely applicable in classroom intervention and the supplementation on manipulative resource materials could provide imaginative learning experiences for the learner.

Above 95 per cent of teachers felt that by using the package mathematical skills among children could be improved, easy to learn methods could be utilized, games in the package provided interesting learning situations and impart adequate computation skills.

The selected teachers, on examining remedial package, also felt that the objectives of remedial teaching were clear (89%), instructional materials on the concept were informative (85%) and that both teachers and parents could successfully use the package on their own (85%).

Developing a Training Module for Primary School Teachers

A major challenge before today's classroom teachers is to deal with L.D. children in regular classroom situations. To meet this challenge effectively, the teachers need to have a thorough understanding of the nature of learning disabilities. As a follow up to the present investigative research, it is advocated that the teachers need to be sensitized on learning disabilities through inclusion of modules in the teacher training-cum-orientation programmes.

Based on the findings of the present study, an attempt has been made by the investigator to develop the following training module for the primary school teachers in the area of learning disabilities with special focus on dyscalculia.

Training Module for Primary School Teachers

Module I		*Rationale*
Unit I	-	Concept, Definition and Type of Learning Disabilities
Unit II	-	Causes, Characteristics and Problems of Learning Disabilities
Module II		*Curriculum*
Unit I	-	Key components in the Identification of Dyscalculic Children
Unit II	-	A Analysis of the Common Errors Committed by Dyscalculic Children
Unit III	-	Examining the Nature of Behavioural Problems Among Dyscalculic Children
Module II		*Strategies and Techniques for Remediation*
Unit I	-	Primary School Mathematics Curriculum. Teachers Attitude and Pedagogical Approach.
Unit II	-	Teaching Techniques Through Use of Remedial Package for Dyscalculic Children
Unit III	-	"Integrated Approach" - A Teaching Strategy.

Incorporation of the above stated module in future training programmes will equip the primary school teachers with the knowledge and skills that would in turn enable children to achieve a strong foundation in mathematics. Agencies and institutions interested in teacher education and in organizing orientation and refresher training can also use this module.

It is hoped that Researchers, Educators, Parents, Allied Health Personnel, Media Representatives and the General Public can together create a powerful team in meeting the needs of this category of L.D. viz., the dyscalculic children. They can work creating a network as analyzers, guidance counsellors and awareness promoters through multipronged approaches. Perhaps the next decade will have greater cheer for these children with better learning environment.

10

Summary and Conclusion

The school is the first and perhaps the most formative formal training ground for any child. Today, while the primary education system in India has expanded into one of the largest in the world, the country also has the dubious distinction of having the world's largest number of out of school children (22 % of the global total). Learning disability of a child might be one of the reasons for dropouts.

Learning disabilities are the most crucial factors in the context of educational profile and achievements. To reduce drop out rate, attention has been directed towards students with learning disabilities by allied health personnel, scientists, educationalists, media representatives and the general public. This interest has helped to foster an environment in which the understanding of learning disabilities has improved dramatically.

The primary school teachers play a pivotal role in the education of L.D. children. The current trend in education of the disabled children is geared toward inclusion. It is, therefore, vital to remediate these children with difficulties in academic subjects by equipping the regular teachers to identify each child's specific problems in learning and correcting them desirably.

Against this backdrop, the investigator designed this study on "Efficacy on Remedial Package in Augmenting Primary School Teachers' Skills to Help Dyscalculic Children". The objectives of the study were to :

Sensitize primary school teachers towards children with learning disabilities

Identify dyscalculics among primary school children

Evolve and implement a remedial intervention programme for dyscalculic children and

Evaluate the efficacy of the remedial package developed.

This research exercise was implemented in four phases. The first phase focused on awareness promotion and training of primary school teachers on learning disabilities, which led to organization of a five day orientation programme for selected teachers on "Identification and Education of Learning Disabled Children".

The second phase laid emphasis on identifying dyscalculic primary school children from selected five matriculation schools based on their achievement across and teachers' opinion on their overall performances in mathematics. This phase also involved the use of various assessment tools to adjudge children's IQ, behaviour problems, arithmetic abilities and neuropsychological process areas among the selected children.

The third phase of the study was exclusively devoted to the preparation of a remedial intervention programme in mathematics, which was implemented for selected experimental group namely dyscalculic children (18) with their teachers as resource personnel.

The fourth and the last phase of the research involved development of remedial package for dyscalculic children for regular use by school teachers in their remedial intervention.

Queries among teachers revealed that a majority of (46 %) was in the age range of 20-30 years; education- wise the group consisted of graduates (65%) and post graduates (29%). As for teaching experience, 53 per cent had 2-4 years followed by 47 per cent with 4-8 years of experience in teaching primary school children. Two to four classes were handled by 41 per cent of the teachers and 36 per cent handled 4-6 classes.

Opportunities for primary school teachers to attend special programmes were found to be very limited. A majority (79%) had no exposure to any sort of in-service training programme.

The findings of the present study are summarized below :

A. Sensitizing Primary School Teachers on Learning Disabilities Among Children

1. Among the various terminologies used in referring to the children with learning difficulties, 50 per cent of the teachers perceived them as 'problem children', 19 per cent as 'educationally backward' and 12 per cent as 'slow learners'. Seven per cent had branded them as 'children with learning disabilities' arbitrarily.
2. Poor teaching (inadequate instruction) in the school (30%) followed by lack of early stimulation (26%) were the causes of

learning disabilities as reported by the teachers.

3. Goal setting for an individual. Individual variation in the degree of learning as a vital factor in making education plans was mentioned by 29 per cent teachers.
4. Amidst heavy load, 73 per cent of the teachers were able to render special attention and 66 per cent were even able to spend two to three hours a week to guide the children with difficulties in learning.
5. Participation in the orientation programme enabled 19 teachers to acquire adequate knowledge of the terminology to refer to the children with learning disability. There was a significant difference at one per cent level between the pre and post mean scores of teachers on their concept of learning disability.
6. Special remedial services in terms of individualized instruction, peer tutoring and the existence of dyslexic remedial training centres had limited awareness among teachers at the pre-training level (58%), while the post-training scores brought forth as much as 90 per cent of the teachers becoming familiar with the above issues. The difference in knowledge scores was significant at five per cent level.

B. Identifying Dyscalculic Primary School Children

7. Academic performance of 1442 primary school children in four major areas of English, Language, Mathematics and Science over a period of one academic year on analysis revealed 20 per cent of low achievers in mathematics, the percentage being more than 25 in classes III, IV and V.
8. The children exhibiting general backwardness in academic subjects were observed to be 47 per cent. The proportion of the children exhibiting difficulties in mathematics was 10 per cent of the selected group.
9. Proportion test (p-test) applied to find out the proportion of girls and boys securing a score of less than 40 in English, Language, Science and Mathematics revealed significant difference at 1 % level only in the case of Language among girls.
10. Among 115 identified as low achievers in mathematics, only 13 per cent were from class I and 15 per cent were in class V. The higher the class, greater was the number of primary school children with difficulties in mathematics. Boys (87) with difficulties in mathematics outnumbered girls (28).

11. A significantly greater number of low achieving children in mathematics had parents at low professional level, low income and low educational levels.
12. Performance of low achievers on Raven's Progressive Matrices revealed that only 34 per cent of these children belonged to 'average intelligence' category, while 41 per cent were grouped under 'below average intelligence', category.
13. Eighty two per cent of the selected low achievers (115) exhibited behaviour problems.
14. Problems related to memory (100) were a significant characteristic stated by the deficits in cognitive domain, auditory processing and poor language (94%).
15. The percentage of children exhibiting behaviour problems among the selected low achievers to mathematics was 87 per cent which is true to the observation that children with learning difficulties do exhibit associated behaviour problems.
16. Arithmetic diagnostic test administered to the low achievers in mathematics revealed that almost 55 per cent had problems in basic arithmetic skills. 19 per cent made inconsistent responses while 17 per cent of them had difficulty in performing higher order tasks.
17. Out of 63 children identified as probab dyscalculics a total of 27 were eliminated, on the grounds of being subnormal in intelligence, underage and normal in their behaviour. Finally, only 36 children were confirmed "dyscalculics".
18. An analysis of arithmetic errors committed by the dyscalculics revealed that a little above 50 per cent of the children had difficulty to bring multiplication tables to memory. Writing the numbers mentioned (42%), wrong operation and problem solving difficulties (each 39%), reading digit-wise (36%), spelling errors and difficulty with written symbols (28%) were observed.
19. The diagnostic test of learning disability to assess neuropsychological problem areas revealed severe problems in the areas of expressive language, cognitive abilities, receptive language and memory among dyscalculics.

C. Remedial Intervention for Dyscalculic Children

20. The effectiveness of the remedial programme through Arithmetic Diagnostic Test revealed significant difference among the control and experimental group, the latter achieving higher mean

scores.

21. Paired 't' test applied to find out the difference in control and experimental group (pre-and post-test scores) revealed significant difference at 1% level. Obviously after the remedial intervention, the performance of experimental group was higher with a mean value (31.16) against the control group mean (15.7) on the arithmetic diagnostic test.

D. Efficacy of Remedial Package Developed for Dyscalculic Children

22. Perusal of the remedial package by the teachers reflected that it was suitable for use in classroom intervention and the manipulative resource materials supplemented could provide imaginative experiences in teaching and learning mathematices. The games introduced and sample sheets on mathematical "probes" were largely appreciated by the teachers.

The investigator has suggested a training module to be considered by teacher training and other related institutes.

Recommendations

Based on the findings of this study, the following recommendations emerge:

- Concerted efforts be made at the National and State levels to subject the primary school curriculum to scientific scrutiny and effect necessary changes in the perspectives, content and methodologies to make it appropriate and developmentally sound for the primary school children.
- Primary school children can learn effectively only from concrete situation. Hence, the primary school teachers' training must be so tailored as to expose them to learn and adopt teaching that facilitates first hand experiences.
- Longitudinal studies on remedial intervention strategy and their effect are needed not only to make them effective for students with learning disabilities but also for all students at risk for failure and lack basic knowledge and skills in mathematics.
- The training on learning disability must be systematically implemented on a war footing, as the sooner it is implemented for all Primary School Teachers, the better it would be for the future of primary education and the progress of the nation.
- One of the immediate tasks for policy makers, administrators and researchers in Special Education Programmes is to create a framework, which clarifies and delineates relevant and standard

terminology relating to learning disabilities.

While the focus of this research was on the general education teachers' planning for students with learning disabilities, a future challenge is to develop successful remedial intervention strategies for secondary teachers so that they can meet the needs of students as a whole and yet provide with the specific instruction needed by students with learning disabilities.

Appendices

Appendix-I

Avinashilingam Institute for Home Science and Higher Education for Women (Deemed University) Coimbatore - 641043

Questionnaire to Elicit Information on the Awareness of Primary School Teachers on Learning Disabilities Among Children

Date:

A. General Information

1. Name of the teacher :
2. Sex : Male/Female
3. Age in years :
4. Name of the school :
5. Medium of instruction :
6. Educational qualification :
7. Years of teaching experience :
8. Class particulars :

Class handled at present	*Subjects taught*	*No. of student in the class*			
		Boys	*Age group*	*Girls*	*Age group*

9. Special seminars / Workshops / Training programmes attended since past five years

S. No.	*Programme*	*Year*	*Organiser*	*Place*	*Duration (No. of days)*

B. Specific Information on Learning Disability

1. Fill up, the following :

1. In a classroom, children differ in the rate of -------------------
2. Primary school teachers must have ----------------- to present academic tasks to learning disabled children
3. The learning disabled child will have ----------------- intelligence
4. Learning disabled children demonstrate-------------------- problems for both visual and auditory stimuli
5. A ------------- center is a must for teaching learning disabled children
6. ----------------- is the first phase to the whole process of remediation of learning disability
7. The goal for behavioural change decided for the learning disabled should proceed from simple to ------------
8. The curriculum programme designed, the materials used and the specific techniques, for the learning disabled should be based on the child's ------ needs

II. Answer the following stating Yes / No :

1. Slow learners are learning disabled children
2. Learning disability may be a condition created by poor teaching
3. Learning disabled children have behavioural problems
4. Mild learning disabled children cannot be integrated with normal children
5. Checklist cannot be used in school for identifying possible learning disabled children
6. Children with learning disability are described as exceptional children
7. In a classroom, informal assessment tools can be used to identify learning disabled children
8. Behavioural problems among learning disabled children cannot be treated

III. Tick the correct answer among the following

1. One of the following methods used in confirming learning disability is
   a. Medical examination
   b. Study of home environment
   c. Intelligence assessment
2. The learning disability of a child can be obvious in the areas of
   a. Reading

b. Writing
c. Arithmetic

3. Medication works well with
   a. Hyperactive learning disabled children
   b. Passive children
   c. Socially withdrawn children
4. A method in teaching learning disabled children is
   a. Verbal explanation followed by demonstration
   b. Demonstration followed by verbal explanation
   c. Verbal explanation and demonstration together
5. For effective teaching, children should be grouped on the basis of
   a. I.Q.
   b. Age
   c. Educational needs
6. Sensory approach used for teaching learning disabled children is
   a. Auditory
   b. Visual
   c. Auditory, visual, tactile and kinesthetic
7. Dyslexic child faces difficulties in
   a. Reading
   b. Arithmetic
   c. Writing
8. In case of learning disability, the child has to be
   a. Neglected
   b. Removed from school
   c. Referred for support

IV. List your answers for the following:

1. Learning disability categories include
   a.
   b.
   c.
2. Possibilities for integrating learning disabled children
   a.
   b.
3. Characteristics of learning disabled children
   a.
   b.
4. Environmental disadvantages leading to learning disability

a.

b.

5. The problems faced by the learning disabled in the classroom

   a.

   b.

6. The remedial method / programmes used for teaching learning disabled children

   a.

   b.

   c.

7. Identification of a learning disabled child can be done by

   a.

   b.

   c.

8. Common psychological problems faced by learning disabled children

   a.

   b.

   c.

Appendix-II

Sensitization Programme on Learning Disabilities Among Children

Organized by

Avinashilingam Institute for Home Science and Higher Education for Women - Deemed University Coimbatore - 641043

Venue - Thiruchitrambalam Auditorium
Date - 07.10.1994
Time - 9.30 a.m.

Sensitization Programme on Learning Disabilities Among Children

Evaluation Proforma

Name of the participant :
Age :
Male / Female :
Educational Qualification :
Designation :
Official Address :
Name of the School if working :
How did you know about this programme?
What are your objectives in attending this programme?
Is this the first programme you have attended on learning disability? Yes No
If yes - state the programme attended
Do you have children with learning problems Yes No
(in your class) Specify type:
List common errors or difficulties faced by the children
How are the children helped?
Do you feel that the children are progressing
Are you interested in participating in a workshop to be organized on learning disabilities
Did you find this programme useful? Yes No
(How)
Give your suggestions for future programmes

Department of Human Development Faculty of Home Science

Avinashilingam Institute for Home Science and Higher Education for Women (Deemed University) Coimbatore - 641043

Cordially invites you for a "Sensitization Programme on Learning Disabilities Among Children"

At 9.30 a.m. on 7th October, 1994

* Concept and Strategies of Learning Disabilities

by

Mrs. Vasanthi Soundarajan M.A., M.Ed. Dip. Sp.Ed. (USA)
Principal
HAL School for Special Education
Bangalore

* Slow Learners and his Educational Needs

by

Miss. Shanthi Gnanavolivu M.A., Sp.Ed. (Denmark)
Principal
Marthomas Special School
Bangalore

Presidential Address :

Dr. (Mrs.) Lakshmi Santa Rajagopal
Vice-Chancellor
Avinashilingam Deemed University
Coimbatore

Venue : Thiruchitrambalam Auditorium

Appendix-III

Arithmetic Diagnostic for Primary School Children

Reading material	*Parameters*						
	Clear print	*Handy*	*Understandable*	*Logical flow*	*Interesting*	*Informative*	*Simple*
1. Leaflet - Concept of learning disability							
2. Booklet - Do you know specific learning disabilities: Terminology and identifiable errors							
3. Pamphlet - Causes of learning difficulties							
4. Flip book - Problems of learning disabled							
5. Folder - Charateristics of learning disabled							
6. Folder - Teaching methods for specific learning disabilities							

Appendix - IV

Arithmetic Diagnostic Test for Primary School Children

S. Ramaa

Reader in Special Education
Regional College of Education (NCERT)
Mysore - 570006
Karnataka State.

Chethana Book House
N.S. Road
Mysore - 24
Karnataka State

Appendix -V

Behavioural Checklist for Screening the Learning Disabled

Dr. Smriti Swarup
Mrs. Dharmishta H. Mehta
Department of Special Education
S.N.D.T. Women's University
Juhu Road
Bombay - 400049

for Examiner's use only

Code No. :
Score :

Teacher ____________________ Student ______________

Name ____________________ Name ______________

Qualifications____________________ Class ______________

Teaching Experience ________ Age ______________

School________________________________

Appendix -VI

Diagnostic Test of Learning Disability

(D.T.L.D)

Test Booklet

Dr. Smriti Swarup
Mrs. Dharmishta H. Mehta
Department of Special Education
S.N.D.T. Women's University
Juhu Road
Bombay - 400049
India

Appendix - VII

REMEDIAL PACKAGE FOR DYSCALCULIC CHILDREN

Appendix-VIII

Checklist to Evaluate the Efficacy of Remedial Package by Primary School Teachers

Teacher's Name:
Class handling :
School :

	Statement	Yes	No
1.	The package helps in achieving the objectives of remedial teaching		
2.	Adequate computation skills for primary school children can be taught using the package		
3.	Information provided in the package is adequate to help dyscalculic children		
4.	Teachers and parents can effectively use the package without orientation		
5.	Games introduced provide interesting learning situations		
6.	Instructional materials on basic concepts of learning disability is informative		
7.	Remedial programme incorporated is largely applicable		
8.	Short cut methods to various concept learning in mathematics is useful		
9.	Manipulative resource material provides imaginative opportunities for concept development		
10.	Parents can be equipped to use the package in helping the dyscalculic child		

Bibliography

Adams, A. (1990). The oral reading errors of readers with learning disability: Variation produced within the instructional and frustrational ranges. Remedial and Special Education. 12 (1) : 48-55.

Adelman, H.S. (1992). Learning disability : The next 25 years. Journal of Learning Disability, 25 (11) : 17-22.

Ahuja, A. (1995). Visible handicaps in the act for the disabled. The Hindu, July 16) 26.

Ahuja, A. (1996). Meeting the needs of learning disabled children : Teacher training. Alpha to Omega Learning Centre. Newsletter (6) : 1-4.

Aiken, L.R. (1970). Attitude towards mathematics. Review of Educational Research 40, 551 - 555.

Akinaso, F.N. (1993). Policy and experiment in mother tongue literacy in Nigeria. International Review of Education, 39(4) : 287.

Alexander, J. (1993). My view on behalf of our children. Today, 22 (1) : 2.

Alexander, K.L., Entwisle, D.R. and Dauber, S.L. (1993). First grade classroom behaviour : Its short and long term consequences for school performance. Child Development, 64 (3) : 801.

Allinder, R.R.M. and Eicher, D.D. (1994). Bouncing back : Regression and recoupment among students with mild disabilities following summer break. Special Services in the Schools, 8 (2) : 129-142.

Aludiapillai (1993). Motivating the teachers, The Hindu, October 26 22.

Anantharaman, Z. and Parthasarathy (1992. October 5). Better life for institutionalized children. The Hindu, 26.

Appasamy, A. (1996. August 27). Leadership qualities in teachers. The Hindu, 26.

Archarya, P. (1988). Search of alternatives in primary education. Journal of Education and Social Change, II (1) : 35.

Arnold, P. and Askew, S. (1993). Handed distribution and figure drawing ability in a deaf school population with severed learning disabilities. The Journal of Child Psychology and Psychiartry and Allied Disciplnes, 4(2): 225

Azad, Y.A. (1990). Research areas in special education. NCTE Bulletin 11(4): 8.

Babu, N.S. (1996. September 10). Remedial teaching. The Hindu, 26.

Baker, J.M. and Zigmond, N. (1990). "Are regular education classes equipped to accommodate students with learning disabilities.

Baksh, S.P. (1996. June 23). Growing out of the curriculum - A question of integration. The Hindu, I.

Balachandran, K. (1993. September 14.) To make the best use of the "Necessary Evil". The Hindu, 3-4.

Balasubramaniam, N. (1996. March 19). Need for academic and organizational autonomy. The Hindu, 26

Bamman, H.A. (1989). Reading. The World Book Encyclopedia, 16: 157-164.

Barrett, M. and Trevett, J. (1991). Attachment Behaviour and the School Child - An Introduction to Educational Therapy, (1st ed.), London, Tavistock, Roultedge, 1.

Barsch, R.H. (1992). Perspectives on learning disabilities, The vectors of a new convergens. Journal of Learning Disabilities, 25(1): 6-8.

Bartel, N.R. (1982). in Mercer, C.D. (1983). Students with Learning Disabilities (2nd ed.), London, Charles, E. Merill Publishing Co., 368

Batchelor, E.S., Gray, J. W. and Dean, R.S. (1990). Emperical testing of a cognitive model to account for neuropsychological functioning underlying arithmetic problem solving. Journal of Learning Disabilities, 23(1): 38-42.

Batchelor, E.S., Gray J.W. and Dean, R.S. (1990). Neuropsychological aspects of arithmetic performance in learning disability. International Journal of Clinical Neuropsychology, 12(2): 90-94.

Bateman, B. (1992). Learning Disabilities: The changing language. Journal of Learning Disability, 25(1): 33.

Bayrd, P. (1996. June). ADHD: Understanding and tips' for parents: Alpha to Omega Learning Centre. Newsletter. (5): 3-4.

Bender, W.N. (1987). Behavioral indicators of temperament and personality in the inactive learner. Journal of Learning Disabilities, 20, 280-306.

Berk, L.E. (1994). Child Development, (3rd ed.), London. Allyn and Bacon, 295.

Bhagat, R. (1993. May 19). Education for all: Tamil Nadu picks up the challenge. Indian Express, 7.

Bhasin, M.P. (1985). The teachers: As behaviourist and perceptualist. Journal of Indian Education, 10(6): 48-50.

Bhatia, A. (1996. November 22-24). Specific Learning Disabilities in Maths: Assessment and Remediation. Report of the National Conference on Learning Disabilities, I-VIII.

Bishop, D.V.M. and Adams, C. (1990). A prospective study of the relationship between specific language impairment, phonological disorders and reading retardation. Jouranal of Child Psychology and Psychiatry, 31(7): 1027-1050.

Blackenship, C.S. (1978). Remediating systematic inversion errors in subtraction through the use of demonstration and feedback. Learning Disability Quarterly, 1, 12-22.

Bond, G.L. and Tucker, M.A. (1979). Reading Difficulties: Their Diagnosis and Correction, New York. Appleton Century Crofts, 406-408.

Bras, P.S. (1980). Ideal school atmosphere. The Educational Review, LXXXVI (4): 69.

Brenan, W. (1982). Changing Special Education, Milton Keynes. The Open University Press, 84.

Brown, D. and Frank, A.R. (1990). "Let me do it", Self monitoring in solving arithmatic problems. Education and Treatment of Children, 13(3): 239-248.

Bruck, M. (1986). Social and Educational Adjustment of Learning Disabled Children. A Review of Issues in Ceci, S.J. (Ed). Handbook of Cognitive, Social and Neurological Aspects of Learning Disabilities, 1, 361-380.

Bryan, T., Donahue, M. and Pearl, R. (1981). Learning Disabled Childrens peer interaction during a small group problem solving task. Learning Disability Quarterly, 4: 13-22.

Cairns, R.B., Cairns, B.D and Neckerman, H.J. (1989). Early school drop out. Configuration and determinants. Child Development, 60(6): 1436.

Carmine, D. (1991). Curricular intervention for teaching higher order thinking to the students: Introduction to the special series. Journal of Learning Disabilities, 24:262-269.

Case, L.P., Harris, K.R. and Graham, S. (1992). Improving the mathematical problem solving skills of students with learning disabilities: Self regulated strategy development. The Journal of Special Education, 26(1).

Cawley (1976). In Mandel C.J. and Gold N (1984). Teaching Handicapped Students, New York, Best Publishing Company, 356.

Cawley, J.F., Fitzmaurice, A.M., Shaw, R., Kolm, H. and Bates, H. (1979). Learning disabled youth and mathematics : A review of characteristics. Learning Disabilities Quarterly, 2(1): 27-44.

Cawley, J.F. and Miller, J.H. (1989). Cross - Sectoral comparisons of the mathematics performance of children with learning disabilities: Are we on the right track towards comprehensive programming. Journal of Learning Disabilities, 22(4): 250-254.

Chalam, K.S. (1996. September 10). Emerging areas of research in primary studies. The Hindu, 26.

Child Asia (1993). Tamil Nadu Makes Primary Education Compulsory. Report of the Sub-committee on Elimination of Child Labour in the Match and Fireworks Industries in Tamil Nadu.

Child's Right Bulletin (1996). Smoking leads to mentally retarded kids. The Child's Right Bulletin, VI(5): 10.

Chopra, R. K. (1991). Status of Teachers in India: Research Note. NCTE Bulletin, III (2 and 3): 10.

Clegg (1972). The Changing Primary School - Its Problems and Priorities - A Statement by Teachers, London, Chatts and Windus.

Crealock, E. and Kronick, D. (1993). Children and Young People with Specific Learning Disabilities. Guide for Special Education, 9, Paris, UNESCO, 1-57.

Daswani, T.C. (1990). Computer based self-learning for children with special needs. NCTE Bulletin, II(4): 9-12.

Department of Special Welfare and UNICEF (1994). The Future is now for the children of Tamil Nadu. Government of Tamil Nadu, 2-6.

Desai, P. (1985). Home variable in learning difficulties of primary school children. Compendium of research. M.S. University of Baroda, III, 66-68.

Desai, A. S. (1989). Education of the child in urban slums: An overview of factors affecting learning and responsive action through social work. The Indian Journal of Social Work, L(4): 509.

Desai, A.N. (1990). Helping the Handicapped - Problems and Prospects New Delhi, Ashish Publishing House, 98-99.

Desai, H. (1994. April 4-6). Family the Anchor of Child. Report of the National Conference on Emerging Horizons in Child Development, New Delhi, ICCW, 112.

Devi, K.S. (1996. May 28). A different use for bamboo sticks in schools. The Hindu, 26.

Diamond, K.E. (1994). Parents who have a child with a disability. Childhood Education, 70(3).

Diamond, K.E., Hesteves, L.L. and O'Connov, C.E. (1994. January). Integrating young children with disabilities, Preschool Problems and Promise. Young Children, 68-75.

Donahue, H., Pearl, R. and Bryan, T. (1982). Learning disabled childrens syntatic proficiency in communication task. Journal of Speech and Hearing Research, 47: 397-403.

DPEP Calling (1995). Kerala's students learning rank incompetence. DPEP Calling, 67(8): 33.

Dudley-Marling, C. (1985). The Pragmatic Skills of Learning Disabled Children: A Review. Journal of Learning Disabilities, 18, pp. 193-199.

Dudley-Marling, C. and Edmiaston, R. (1985). Social Status of Learning Disabled Children and Adolescents: A Review. Learning Disabled Quarterly, 18: 189-204.

Eccler (1989). Avoid the 'Coattrack' Syndrome. Christian science monitor. The Hindu, Science and Children Section.

Elia, J., Welsh, P.A., Gullotta, C.S. and Rapoport, J.L. (1993). Academic performance. Journal of Psychology and Psychiatry and Allied Disciplines, 34(5): 785.

Emmanuel, A. (1996. September 26). Teachers who make a difference. The Hindu, III.

Epstein, H.H. and Cullihan, D. (1984). Behaviour problems of mildy handicapped and normal adolescents. Journal of Clinical Child Psychology, 13: 33-34.

Esser, G., Sdimidt, M.H. and Woerner, W. (1990). Epidemiology and course of psychiatric disorders in school age children - Results of a longitudinal study. Journal of Child, Psychology and Psychiatry, 31(2): 243-263.

Falchikov, N. (1993). Attitudes and values of lecturing staff: Tradition, innovation and change. Higher Education, 25(4): 488.

Fantasia, K. (1981). An investigation of formal analysis as an intervention to improve word problem computation for learning disabled children in Lovitt, B.S. (1989). Introduction to Learning Disabilities, London, Alyn and Bacon Inc., 292-396.

Farr, R. (1989). Dyslexia. The World Book Encyclopedia :London. World Book Inc., 5, 357, 398.

Fernandez, M.D. (1992. July 7). Their's a difficult role. The Hindu, 26.

Fleischner, J.E. Nuzum, M.B. and Marzola, E.S. (1987). Devising an instructional programme to teach arithmetic problem solving skills to students with learning disabilities. Journal of Learning Disabilities, 20: 214-217.

Gakhar, S. (1983). Study of the effect of socio-economic status on the mathematical achievement of eight grade children. Journal of the Institution of Educational Research, 7(2): 27.

Gakhar, S.C. (1986). Home variables as determinants of mathematical concept learning. Experiments in Education, XIV(6): 97.

Ganapathy, M. and Singh, R. (1981). The impact of socio-economic conditions of achievement. Experiments in Education, IX(8) : 144.

Ganesan, L. (1995. August 29). Child oriented education. The Hindu, 26.

Gautam, V.K. (1991). Inquiry training model of teaching. The Primary Teacher, XVI(1): 13.

Gearheart, B.R. and Gearheart, C.J. (1989). Learning Disabilities: Educational Strategies, (5th ed.), London, Merill Publishing Company, 337-366.

Geary, D.C., Widaman, K.F. Little, T.D. and Cormier, P. (1987). Cognitive addition: Comparison of learning disabled and academically normal elementary school children. Cognitive Development, 2(3) 249-269.

George, V.D. and Sanandraj, S.H. (1983). Some adjustmental traits of behavioural problem students. Journal of Institute of Educational Research, 7(3): 38.

Gersten, R. and Kelly, B. (1992). Coaching secondary special education teachers in implementation of a innovative videodisc mathematics curriculum.

Ghose, S. (1996. June 23). Going out of the curriculum: Mere droplets. The Hindu II.

Gokaran, N.A. (1989). The needs of children and school social work services. The Indian Journal of Social Work. L(4): 03-404.

Gonsalvez, E.R. (1994. November 7-11). Teachers as facilitators: Report of the National Conference on Learning Disabilities, Madras, 43.

Gopal, M. (1995. July). Metaphors and images of teaching DPEP calling. DPEP Newsletter, (6, 7 & 8): 22-23.

Gopalakrishnan, S. (1992. September 8). Smoother not the joys of children. The Hindu, 26.

Govt. of India (1993). National Plan of Action for the SAARC Decade of the Girl Child 1991 - 2000 A.D. Govt. of India Dept. of Women and Child Development, New Delhi. Ministry of Human Resource Development, 12 and 13.

Greenleaf, C., Hill, G. and Rally, B. (1994). Learning from our diverse students: Helping teacher rethink problematic teaching and learning. Teaching and Teacher Education, 10(5): 521-524.

Greshan, F.M. (1982). Misguided mainstreaming: The cost for social skills training with handicapped children. Exceptional Children, 48: 422-433.

Crolnick, N.S. and Slowiaczek, M.L. (1994). Parents involvement in children's schooling. A multidimensional conceptualization and motivational model. Child Development, 65(1): 237-252.

Gupta, S.P. (1996). Improvement of standard's - An abiding concern of UGC. Journal of Higher Education, 19(1): 43.

Haeri, D. (1994). Preparing children for school Education Child Asia, (12): 22.

Hallahan, D.P. (1992). Some thoughts on why the prevalence of learning disabilities has increased. Journal of Learning Disabilities, 25(8): 523-528.

Harris, J.R. and Liebert, R.M. (1987). The Child - Development from Birth through Adolescence, (2nd ed.), New Jersey, Prentice Hall Inc., 408, 419.

Hayes, M.L. (1995). Social Skills: The bottom line for adult learning disability success. Madras Dyslexia Association. Newsletter, 1(2): 4

Heward, W.L. and Orlansky, M.D. (1986). Exceptional Children: An Introductory Survey to Special Education, London. Charles E. Merill Publishing Company, 102-105. Heward, W.L. and Orlansky, M.D. (1986). Exceptional Children: An Introductory Survey to Special Education, (3rd. ed.). Columbus, Merill Publishing, Company.

Hills, T.W. (1993). Assessment in context - Teachers and Children at work. Young Children, 48(5): 21-25.

Hitch, G.J. and McAuley, E. (1991). Working memory in children with specific arithmatical learning difficulties. British Journal of Psychology, 82, 375.

HUDCO (1994). Housing and Urban Development Corporation. Housing and Finance, Publication Division, New Delhi, Patiala house, 232.

ICCW (1994. April 4-7). Indian Council for Child Welfare: Report of the Conference of Emerging Horizons in Child Development, ICCW, New Delhi, 4.

Illango, M.S. (1996. July 16). An accepted teacher. The Hindu, 26.

Indra, V. (1990. October 7). A fast - paced childhood. The Hindu, 19.

Ismail, R.S. (1996). Universalising Primary Education (UPE) By 2000 - Can India Make it? UNICEF Report. The UPE File 96/01.

Jangira, N.K. (1990). Quality teaching for all. NCTE Bulletin, II(4): 13-14.

Jangira, N.K. (1991). UNESCO initiative on special needs in the classroom. NCTE Bulletin, III(2-4): 9.

Jaya, N. and Geetha, T. (`1994. December 13). Learning Disabilities among children. The Hindu, 26.

Jayakumar, K. (1997. June 17). Change the classroom. The Hindu, 26.

Jagathabal, K. (1997. May 14). Teaching mathematics. The Hindu, 26.

Jenkins J.R., Jewell, M., Leicester, N., O' Conner, R.E., Jenkis, L.M. and Troutner, (1994). Accommodation for individual differences without classroom ability group: An experiment in school restructuring. Exceptional Children, 60(4): 344-358.

Jimenenz, G.J. (1992). Operational structures and arithmetic performance. Children with Learning Difficulties, Revista - dec, psiocologica - General - Y - Aphicde. 45(2): 211-217.

Jitendra, A.K. and Hoff, K. (1996). The effects of schema based instruction

on the mathematical word problem solving performance of students with learning disabilities. Journal of Learning Disabilities, 29(4): 422.

John, P. (1995. March 12). Is your child smart or slow - The Week 31.

Jordan, N.C., Levine, S.C. and Hultenlocher, J. (1995). Calculation abilities in young children with different patterns of cognitive functioning. Journal of Learning Disabilities, 28(1): 53-64.

Joseph, A. (1985). Educational problems of socially disadvantaged children. Journal of Indian Education, 11(1): 14.

Joshua, (1996. June 23). Growing out of curriculum, A question of integration. The Hindu, II.

Joshua, K. (1996. June 23). Human brain - leftist - or rightist. The Hindu, VIII.

Kajjari, J.N. and Khadi, P.B. (1994). Factors influencing study habits and study involvement. Indian Psychological Review, 42(-6) 1.

Kanniyan, S. (1997. June 24). The emergence of a unique learning system. The Hindu, 26.

Kannappn, D.I. (1995. May 16). Competency based training. The Hindu, 26.

Katz, L.G. (1993). Prizing diversity. Young Children, 48(5): 2.

Kaul, M.L. (1986). Obedience and school children. Journal of Indian Education, 11(6): 48.

Kaul, S. (1996. February 28). Area of darkness. The Hindustan Times, 9.

Kavanogh, J.F. and Truss, T.J. (1988). Learning Disabilities. Proceedings of the International Conference of Learning

Disabilities, 253-256.

Kelly, B., Gersten, R. and Carnine, D. (1990) Student name error patterns as a function of curriculum design: Teaching fractions to remedial high school students with learning disabilities. Journal of Learning Disabilities, 23(1): 23.

Khan, A. (1995). Why teachers dissatisfaction? Its an occupational hazard, School, II(4): 12.

Khurana, G.S. (1988). Students (Class IX-X) of Ludhiana: School Adjustment problems. Journal of Indian Education, 14(1): 21.

Kirby, J.R. and Becker, L.D. (1988). Cognitive components of learning problems in arithmetic. Remedial and Special Education, 9(5): 7-15.

Kirk, S.A. (1970). Education Exceptional Children, New Delhi, IBH Publishing. Co. 262-272.

Kirk, S.A., and Elkins, J. (1975). Characteristics of children enrolled in the cult service demonstration centres, Journal of Learning Disabilities, 8: 267 and 630-637.

Kishore, L. (1984). Individual guidance - An aid in learning: The Educational Review, XV(1): 1.

Kothari, C.R. (1996). Research Methodology, Methods and Techniques, (2nd ed.), Vishwal Prakashan.

Kothari, S. (1994). Some Problems of Education, Science and Development, C. Subramaniam Birthday Felicitations volume, Madras, Orient Longman Ltd., 158.

Kosc, L. (1974). Developmental dyscalculia. Journal of Learning Disabilities, 7: 164-177 and 267.

Koscinski, S.T. and Gast, D.L. (1993). Use of constant time delay in teaching multiplication facts to students with learning disabilities. Journal of Learning Disabilities, 26(8): 533-44, 567.

Kousalaya, S. (1992. September 20). Overcoming handicaps in learning. The Hindu, X.

Krishnamurthy, K.G. (1994. April 4-7). The child in India's development plans. Report of the National Conference on Emerging Horizons in Child Development, ICCW, New Delhi.

Kulak, A.G. (1993). Parallels between maths and reading disability: Common issues and approaches. Journal of Learning Disabilities, 26(10): 666-673.

Kumar, M. (1985). Language ability and acquisition of mathematics concepts at primary school level. Experiments in Education, XIII(5): 81.

Lakshman, P. (1996. January 30). Students assistance programme. The Hindu, 26.

Larry, B.S. (1989). Learning Disabilities, Psychological Abstract, 76(11); 35-37.

Lefrancois, G. R. (1983). OF Children, (4th ed.) Blemount, California, Woodsworth Publishing Company, p. 385.

Leon, J. and Pepe, H. (1983). Self instructional training: Cognitive behaviour modification for remediating arithmetic deficits. Exceptional Children, 50: 54-61.

Lerner, J., Ozudnowski, C.M. and Goldenberg, D. (1981). Special Education for Early Childhood Years, New Jersey, Prentice Hall Inc., 47-49.

Lerner, J. (1989). Learning Disabilities: Theories Diagnosis and Teaching Strategies, (5th ed.), Boston. Houghton Mifflin Company, 430-465.

Lewis, C., Hitch, G.J. Walker, P. (1994). The prevalence of specific arithmetic difficulties and specific reading difficulties in 9 to 10 years old, boys and girls. Journal of Child Psychiatry, 35(2): 283-292.

Light, J.G. and Defries, J.C. (1995). Comorbidity of reading and mathematics disabilities: Genetic and environmental etiologies. Journal of Learning Disabilities, 28(2): 96-106.

Lombordo, T.W. and Drabman, R.S. (1985). Teaching learning disabled children multiplication tables. Academic Therapy, 20(4): 437-442.

Loveland, K.A., Fletcher, J.M. and Bailey, V. (1990). Verbal and non-verbal communication of events in learning disability subtypes. Journal of Clinical and Experimental Neuropsychology, 12(4): 433-447.

Lovitt, J.C., Smity, D., Kidder, J. and Evison, R. (1974). Using Arranged Programmed Events to alter Substraction Performance of Children with Learning Disabilities in Lovitt, T.C. (1989). Introduction to Learning Disabilities, London, Allyn and Bacon.

Lovitt, T.C. (1989). Introduction to Learning Disabilities, London, Allyn and Bacon Inc., 292-296.

McKay,T.A.W.N. and Boyle, J.M. (1994). Meeting the needs of pupils with learning difficulties. What do primary and secondary schools expect of their education psychologists? Educational Research, 36(2): 187.

Magne, O. (1978). The psychology of remedial mathematics. Didakomtry, (59): 27.

Malavika, A. (1995). Mental Health of Indian Children, New Delhi, Sage Publications.

Mani, M.N.G. (1986). Integrated education of the visually disabled - A perspective toward 2000 A.D. Integrated Education of Disabled, 4(3): 22.

Mary, A.L. (1995). Schools have to think hard and change practices. School, III(2): 8.

Mathew, M.C. (1996. November 21-24). Development monitoring of children during the school years. Report of the National Conference on Learning Disabilities, Madras, 3, 1-4.

Matsuura, M., Okubo, Y., Kojima, T., Takahashi, R., Wang, Y.F. Shen, Y.C. and Lee, C.K. (1993). A gross national prevalence: Study of children with emotional and behavioural problems. Journal of Child Psychology and Psychiatry and Allied Disciplines, 34(3): 307.

Mclntosh, R., Vanghn, S., Schumm, J.S., Haager, D. and Lee, O. (1993). Observations of students with learning disabilities in general education classrooms. Exceptional Children, 60(3): 249-261.

McKay, H. (1994. November, 7-11). Specific learning difficulties. Report of National Conference on Learning Disabilities, Madras, 7.

Menon, S. V. (1991). Effect of enriched learning and improved recreation on the psychological development of under achievers. Experiments in Education, XII(8): 211.

Menon, L. (1994. November 26). Time to check dyslexia among kids. Indian Express, 8.

Menon. L. (1995. March 18). Dyslexia cripples children in Kerala. Indian Express, 9.

Mercer, C.D. (1983). Students with Learning Disabilities, (2nd ed.) London, Charles, E. Merill Publishing House, 340-350.

Mercer, C.D. and Miller, S.P. (1992). Teaching students with learning problems in math to acquire, understand and apply basic math facts. Remedial and Special Education, 13(3): 19-35.

Milton, G.D. (1993 August 24). Punishment and emotional training. The Hindu, 26.

Mitchell, A.L. (1993). Shouldn't preschool people advocate for better elementary school too? Young Children, 48(5): 58-60.

Misra, N. (1996. January 19). A tough struggle to maintain standards, Education: Indian classrooms. India Abroad, 8.

Mohan, J. and Gulati, A. (1986). Academic achievement - A review of determinants. Indian psychological Review, 30(4)): 1-2.

Mornoe, E.E. and Panchyshyn, R. (1995). Vocabulary considerations for teaching mathematics. Childhood Education - Infancy through childhood, 72(2); 80-83.

Montague, M. (1991). Teaching Verbal Mathematics Problem Solving Skills to Students, in Communication Skills and Classroom Success. Assessment and Therapy, Methodologies for Language and Learning Disabled Students. Simon, C.S. (Ed). Ean Claire Thinking Publishers, 434-440.

Muthukumaran, S. (1995). Teacher effectiveness. University News, XXXIII (11): 8.

Murthy, V.K. (1995. April 18). Slow Learning Children - A review. The Hindu, 26.

Nabuzoka, D. and Smith, P.K. (1993). Sociometric status and social behaviour of children with or without learning difficulties. Journal of Child Psychology and Psychiatry, 34(8): 1435-1448.

Narayan, J. (1994. November 7-11). Feasibility of education of children with specific learning disabilities in Indian educational set up. Report of the National Conference on Learning Disabilities, Madras, 26-27.

Narayan, J. and Menon, K. (1989). Organisation of Special Class in a Regular School, Secunderabad. National Institute for Mentally Handicapped, 1.

Narayan, R. (1994. October 22). Issues in implementations of child care services, policy for the young child in Tamil Nadu. Report of the Seminar, Proceedings, 10, Madras, M.S. Swaminathan Research Foundation, 15-19.

Narayanan, S. (1994. November 7-11). A successful dyslexic student name - A case study presentation. Report of the National Conference on Learning Disabilities, 33-37.

Narayanan, K.S. (1997. July 1). A good teacher is the answer. The Hindu, 26.

NCERT (1995). National Council for Educational Research and Training, Students learning level raises more questions than answers! How reliable is it? School, III(4): 10.

NCERT (1997). Study of Physical Health, Learning, Emotional and Behavioural Problems Among Primary School Children in Mandya District, Mysore Regional Institute of Education, 17.

NCTE (1990). Special Education - New challenges. NCTE Bulletin, II(4):1.

Newman, R.S. (1989). Asian Studies Association of Australia - South Asia Publications Series, 4, New Delhi. Sterling Publishers, 1.

NIPCCD (1994). Counselling and guidance, Orientation for the principals of schools in Delhi. NIPCCD Newsletter, 15(3): 15-16.

NJCLD (1987). National Joint Committee on Disabilities , Learning Disabilities: Issues on definitions. Journal of Learning Disabilities, 20, 107.

NPE, POA (1992). National Policy on Education, Plan of Action, Department of Education, Ministry of Human Resource Development, New Delhi, NCERT.

Pandey, R.S. and Advani (1995). Perspectives in Disability and Rehabilitation, (1st ed.). New Delhi. Vikas Publishing House, 1-215.

Pangotra, N.N. (1986). School drop outs: A crucial problem. Journal of Indian Education, 12(2): 42.

Parmer, R.S. and Cawley, J.F. (1991). Challenging the realities and passivity that characterize arithmatic instruction for children with mild handi- caps. Remedial and Special Education, 5(2): 23.

Parmer, R.S. and Cawley, J.F. Mecer, J.H. (1994). Difference in mathematics performance between students with learning disabilities and students with mild retardation. Exceptional Children, 60(6): 549-564.

Patyal, C.B. (1980). A study on the effect of low and high readability materials on the reading comprehension of students in the context of reading abilities. Journal of the Institution of Educational Research, 4(2): 35.

Peer, L. (1996. March 17). Helping the dyslexic child. The Sunday Times of India, 11.

Philip, J. (1996. November 22-24). Learning disabilities from health to education. Report of the National Conference on Learning Disabilities, Madras, 21-III.

Pillawalla, N. (1993. June). Educating tomorrow's students. Young Mother, 12-14.

Podder, S. (1996. November 21-14). "Hands - On experience of mathematical concepts." Report of the National Conference on Learning Disabilities, Madras, 5, I.

Prakash, V. (1996. August 27). Mathematics - Sweet and sour. The Hindu, 26. Prasad, B. (1982). Relationship of constitutional factors to learning difficulties among primary school children. Indian Educational Review, 17(2): 1.

Pressley, M. Sigmons, S. Synder, B. and Cariglia, B.T. (1989). Strategy instruction, research comes of age". Learning Disabilities Quarterly, 12:16-30.

Radhakrishnan, L. (1996). Diagnosis and Remediation of Arithmatic Disabilities, in Ramaa, S. (Ed.) Package on Learning Disability, Mysore, Regional College of Education, NCERT, 5.

Rajaiah, B. (1990). School organization and teachers. The Educational Review, LXXXVI(4): 64.

Rajasekaran, S. (1996. August). Innovations in learning mathematics. The Hindu, 26.

Rajput, J.S. (1996. March 19). Teacher's training for inclusive schools. The Hindu, 26.

Ramaa, S. (1992). Handbook on Learning Disabilities, Mysore Regional College of Education, NCERT, 1-40.

Ramaa, S. (1993). Diagnosis and Remediation of Dyslexia: An Emperical Study in Kanada - An Indian Language, Mysore, Vidyasagar Publications.

Ramaa, S., (1994). Arithmetic Diagnostic Test for Primary School Children, Mysore, Chethana Book House.

Ramaa, S. (1996). General Characteristics and Behaviour Manifestations of Learning Disabilities. Package on Learning Disabilities, Mysore, Regional Institute of Education, NCERT.

Ramachandran, K.(1996. June 1). State wide school enrollment drive underway. The Hindu, 4.

Ramanujam, L. (1994. November 7-11). Young adults with learning disabilities. Report of the National Conference on Learning Disabilities, Madras, 38.

Ramanujam, L. (1995. August 8-12). Learning to read and reading to learn. Report of the National Seminar on Learning Disabilities, Bangalore.

Ramanujam, L. (1996). Sensory integration - Alpha to Omega learning center. Newsletter, 5:6.

Rani, MVU and Bhadramani, G. (1993). Child abuse in schools. Experiments in Education, 21(9): 231-236.

Rao, Y.R. (1988). The study of the learning disabilities of rural children. Journal of the Institution of Educational Research, 12(1): 1-10.

Rao, D.B. (1994). Teachers' role in dealing with learning disabilities. Journal of Educational Research and Extension, 30(4): 218.

Rao, C.I.V. (1996. May 14). Lack of response to educational commissions. The Hindu, 26.

Rao, C.G. (1997. June 24). Kindle the creative spirit in students. The Hindu, 26.

Rao, V.N. and Parthasarathy, R. (1995). Problems teacher's don't appreciate. School, III(2) 8.

Rao, V.N. and Parthasarathy, R. (1996. November 12). Anatomy of classroom discipline. The Hindu, 26.

Ravens, J.C. (1965). Coloured Progressive Matrices, London, ET Heron and Co. Ltd.

Reisman, R. and Kauffman, S.(1980). Teaching Mathematics to Children with Special Needs, Columbus CH Merill.

Resnick, L.B. (1983). A development theory of number understanding: In H.P. Ginsburg (Ed.). The Development of Mathematical Thinking, New York, Academic Press, 105-151.

Rourke, B.P. and Strang, J.D. (1983). Subtypes of reading and arithmetic disabilities: A neuropsychological analysis in Rutter, M.J. (Ed.). Developmental Neuropsychology, New York, Guilford Press, 473-488.

Rourke, B.P. (1993). Arithmetic disabilities, specific and otherwise: A neuropsychological perspective. Journal of Learning Disabilities, 26(4): 214-226.

Rourke, B.P. and Deldetto, J.E. (1994). Learning Disabilities: A Neuropsychological Perspective. In Kazdin, A.E. (Ed.).

Developmental Clinical Psychology and Psychiatry Series, New Delhi, Sage, 30.

Rush, S. and Vitale, P.A. (1994). Analysis for determining factors that place elementary students at risk. Journal of Educational Research, 87(6): 325-332.

Rutter, M. (1995). Education and mental health, The role of schools. World Health, 28.

Sacheendran, A. (1996. November 22-24). Services for children with learning disabilities. Report of the National Conference of Learning Disabilities, Madras, 32-I.

Santhanam, K. (1992. September 20). Overcoming handicaps in learning. The Hindu, XI.

Sarangi, H. (1989). Learning Disabilities: A psycho educational perspective. Disabilities and Impairments, 3(1): 38-46.

Sarojini Devi, P. (1997, July 1). Teacher training warrants scrutiny. The Hindu, 26.

Scarborough (1990). Very Early Language Deficits in Dyslexic Children. Child Development, 61(6): 1728-1743.

Scary, D.C. (1990). A componential analysis of an early learning deficit in mathematics. Journal of Experimental Child Psychology, 49(3): 363-383.

Schiller, P. and Rossano, J. (1988). Preparing your young child for school. PTA Today, 13(7): 11 and 12.

Schumn, J.S., Vanghn, S., Hagger, D., McDowell, J., Rothlin, L. and Saumell, L. (1995). General education teacher planning : What students with learning disabilities expect?. Exceptional Children, 61(4): 335-352.

Sethia, P., Sinha, S.P. and Saxena, S. (1994). Controlled processing among learning disabled children. Disabilities and Impairments, 8(1): 1-8.

Sewell, G. (1986). Coping with Special Needs: A Guide for New Teachers, London, Croom Helm, Ltd.

Shalve, R.S. and Gross, T.V. (1993). Development dyscalculia and medical assessment. Journal of Learning Disabilities, 26(2): 134-137

Shamsuddin (1991). Teachers role in a changing society. The Primary Teacher XVI(1): 8.

Share, D.L., Moffitt, T.E. and Silva, P.A. (1988). Factors associated with arithmetic and reading disability and special arithmetic disability. Journal of Learning Disabilities, 21(5): 313-320.

Sharma, G. (1993. September 19). Tackling learning disabilities. The Hindu, V. Shields, D. (1989). Learning Disability, The World Book Encyclopedia, London, World Book, Inc., 12: 165-166.

Silver, A.A. and Hagin, R.A. (1990). Disorders of Learning in Childhood, New York, John Wiley and Sons, 35-38.

Singh, K.R.P. (1986). Preparing better teachers. Journal of Indian Education, 12(2): 3.

Singh, R.D. Ahluwalia, S.P. and Verma, S.K. (1994). A study of attitude of high school students towards mathematics. Experiments in Education, XIII(10): 207-213.

Singhal, R.P. (1987) Class size: Is the smaller the better? Perspectives in Education, 3(2): 87-103.

Singhal, S. (1990). Effective and ineffective teachers - Do students differentiate? Perspectives in Education, 6(3): 237.

Singhal, S.P. (1988). Significance of behaviour modification techniques in classroom settings. Journal of Indian Education, 14(4): 63.

Sinha, S.P. (1991). Behaviour modification in classroom setting. The Primary Teacher, XVI(4): 18-26.

Sodhi, S. (1990). Dyslexia - A Step in the Right Direction, Madras Dyslexia Association, Madras.

Sohoni, N.K. (1990). The school system making hostages of children. ICCW News Bulletin, XXXVIII(3): 29.

Srinivasan, P.K. (1994). No head for numbers. The Hindu, Sunday Magazine, V.

Srivastava, R.V. (1995. August 29). Making learning compulsory work. The Hindu, 26.

Starr, J.W. (1969). The Teaching of Mathematics in the Elementary School, Pernnsylva. International Text Book Company.

Stevenson, J., Pennington, Browning, F. Gilger, J.W., Defies, J.C. and Gillis, J.J. (1993). Hyperactivity and spelling disability: Testing for shared genetic etiology. The Journal of Child Psychology and Psychiatry, 37(7): 1137.

Subramanyam, S. (1986). Reading, writing and arithmetic scores as predictors of academic success in primary school children. Experiments in Education, XIII(11): 195-200.

Sugai, G. and Smith, P. (1986). The equal addition method of subtraction taught with a modeling technique. Remedial and Special Education, 791: 40-48.

Sumangala, V. (1995). Some psychological variables discriminating between high and low achievers in mathematics. Experiments in Education, XXIII(10 and 11): 173.

Sutherland, P. (1993). A cognitive development study of the ability to add and subtract among children with learning difficulties in maths. Early Child Development Care, 95(41-48).

Swaminathan, M.S. (1994. October 22). Policy for the young child in Tamil Nadu. Report of a seminar, Proceedings 10, Madras, M.S. Swaminathan Research Foundation, 7.

Swanson, H.C. (1994). The role of working memory and dynamic assessment in the classification of children with learning disabilities. Learning Disabilities Research and Practice, 9(4): 190-202.

Swarup, S. and Mehta, D.H. (1991). Behavioural Checklist for Screening the Learning Disabled. Bombay, SNDT Women's University.

Swarup, S. and Mehta, D.H. (1992). Diagnostic Test of Learning Disability (DTLD). Bombay, SNDT Women's University.

Thomas, C.C. Englert, C.S. and Gregg, S. (1987). An analysis of errors and strategies in the expository writing of learning disabled students. Remedial and Special Education, 8(1): 21-30.

Ujjwalarani, M.V. and Kumari, S.B. (1994). The teachers we like and dislike - Pupils conceptions of their teachers. Experiments in Education, XXII (3): 55.

UNICEF (1988). The Child in South Asia - Issues in Development as if Children Mattered, New Delhi, UNICEF.

UNICEF (1996). Universal Primary Education UPE By 2000 - Can India Make it?. The HPE File Report - 96/01.

Vaidynathan, S. (1995). Itinerant Teacher. Madras Dyslexia Association. Newletter, 1(2): 7.

Van - Houten, R. and Rolider, A. (1990). The use of colour mediation techniques to teach number identification and single digit multiplication problems to children with learning problems. Education and Treatment of Children, 13(3): 216-225.

Venketaramana, T.S.R. (1995. December 19). An overdue legislation to help the disabled. The Hindu, 25.

Venketaramana, D (1996. January 23). Right brain oriented curriculum for all round developmment. The Hindu, 26.

Venugopal, G. (1994). Cognitive style and achievement of pupils. Experiments in Education, XXXII(9): 187.

Venugopal, G. (1994). Intellect profile and advancement of middle school pupils. Experiments in Education, XXII(7): 141.

Weldon, M. (1996). Promoting self esteem, Alpha to Omega learning center. Newsletter, (6): 5.

Witt, J.C., Elliot, S.N., Greshman, F.M., Kramer, J.J. (1988). Assessment of Special Children: Tests and Problem Solving Process, London Scot. Forsman and Company.

Woodward, J. and Howard, L. (1994). The misconceptions of youth: Errors and their mathematical meaning. Exceptional Children, 61(2): 126-136.

Wolff, S. (1989). Childhood and Human Nature - The Development of Personality, (Ist ed.), London. Routledge, 22.

Wong, B. (1985). Metacognition and Learning Disabilities in Weller, T. G., Forrest, P.D. and Mackunnon, E. (Ed.). Metacognition and Human Performance, New York, Academic Pres, 137-180.

World Bank Sector Review (1995). Priorities and strategies for education. DPEP Calling, A DPEP Newsletter, 36.

Yashodhara, K. (1996). Identification of Children with Learning Disabilities. Package on Learning Disability, Mysore, Regional Institute of Education (NCERT), 24.

Index

G

H

I

J

K

L

M